Wine at the End
of the Feast

Wine at the End of the Feast

Embracing
Spiritual Change
as We Age

KRISTEN JOHNSON INGRAM, O.S.A.

LOYOLAPRESS.

CHICAGO

LOYOLAPRESS.

3441 N. ASHLAND AVENUE
CHICAGO, ILLINOIS 60657
(800) 621-1008
WWW.LOYOLABOOKS.ORG

Cover and interior design by Megan Duffy Rostan
Cover illustration: Susie Weber

Library of Congress Cataloging-in-Publication Data
Ingram, Kristen Johnson.
    Wine at the end of the feast : the spirituality of aging / Kristen
Johnson Ingram.
        p. cm.
Includes bibliographical references.
    ISBN 0-8294-1936-5
    1. Christian aged—Religious life. 2. Aging—Religious aspects—
Christianity. 3. Church work with the aged. 4. Aging—Social
aspects. I. Title.
    BV4580.I54 2003
    248.8'5—dc21   2003008430

Printed in the United States of America
    07 08 09 10 Bang 10 9 8 7 6 5 4 3

In memory of my grandmothers,
Elizabeth Stephens Metcalfe and
Jessie McJunkin Johnson,
who showed me how to age
without getting old.

Contents

PART III: STEPS IN THE JOURNEY

PART IV: TO SEE THEE FACE TO FACE

Foreword

SOMETIME IN THE 1970S, A FRIEND, A psychiatrist, handed me a copy of *The Art of Living Long*, which he had found in the reserve section of a medical school library. "I think you'll find this very interesting," he said. Since it was, as I recall, fewer than one hundred pages long, I read it right away. It was very interesting, just as he said. Though I didn't get to read it for a second time before my friend had to return it and have never been able to find another copy, *The Art of Living Long* is one of the books that keeps me thinking about the way I live my life in this world.

Since I read *The Art of Living Long* thirty or more years ago, I don't remember all the facts about it. I think it was written more than four hundred years ago by an Italian engineer. I think his name was Luigi Cornearo. I'm absolutely sure that he was older than one hundred when he died. His thesis was that life is divided, roughly, into four quarters. At the beginning of the third quarter (age fifty), one goes into physical, intellectual, emotional, and spiritual training for the fourth quarter, which begins at age seventy-five. At age seventy-five, one has made a place for himself in society. One knows who he is—and who he isn't—and, given what he knows about himself, what he can yet become. What one can yet become is the prime motivation in old age. And given all the conditioning of body, mind, and spirit during the third quarter of life, one is still in good, maybe robust, health. Furthermore, one may have wealth or, at least, some sources of income that no longer require employment. So now it's time to give one's life away, for the good of others, for family, for friends, for community, for society, for the whole world. Beyond the search for identity and probably beyond the struggle for economic stability, one is now free to become and free to share, to serve—indeed, to squander wisdom and love on the world as never before in life. At seventy-five, one is still becoming. At eighty, becoming still. And on and on.

As I was reading Kristen Ingram's book *Wine at the End of the Feast,* all of that came back to me. Long life is a good thing under most circumstances. Few people want life over soon. But there's one thing that doesn't enhance life, and that's the denial of—and, therefore, the obsession with—physical death. Everyone is going to die, though no one knows exactly when or how. Paradoxically, the frank and forthright acceptance of it—even the embracing of it—takes death's "dominion" (anxiety, fear, depression, hopelessness) away. The years, months, weeks, and days of remaining life aren't just a long waiting for resurrection after physical death. Every day is the day of resurrection, after "the little death of sleep." Alleluia! There's another day in which to become by loving the world and everything and everyone in it. That's the spirituality Kristen Ingram is proclaiming. Resurrection, she says, is what one is destined for, and that destiny can be realized today. In every activity of everyday life—and in all inactivity, even on one's deathbed—one continually "invites God to occupy [the] heart." Those dualisms with which we've been conditioned to live (body versus soul, human versus divine, time versus eternity, earth versus heaven) are dispelled, so that all is one in the heart occupied by God. The result is freedom, is joy in everything and everyone—though not in evil, which one joyfully resists. And that's why the elderly can so often be seen on the frontline of the battle between Good and Evil and, better yet, are practiced, patient, and wise peacemakers.

I've known and greatly admired Kristen Ingram for many years. She's a martyr. By that I mean that she's a bold and unabashed witness to the resurrection of Jesus

Christ and to the life of resurrection with Jesus Christ. Lucky for us, Kristen, I suspect, has never had a thought she kept to herself. That would be selfish. She'll talk about it. She'll write about it. She'll just give herself away, fearless of judgment. What comes to her as a gift she gives to others as a gift. *Wine at the End of the Feast* is one of her many gifts to us. Some paragraphs can be scanned. Some have to be reread and thought about for a while. Then there are those lovely short sentences that contain the human/divine wisdom that one can find in the Wisdom Literature and the Gospels. She knows herself; she knows us; she knows God in herself and in us. Only time will make this judgment, but I'm quite comfortable in mentioning her in the same breath as, say, Julian of Norwich or Margery Kempe or Evelyn Underhill. What I am sure of is that, in Eugene, Oregon, there's a woman who, at every moment, invites God to occupy her heart and will do so, with characteristic insistence, at the moment of death.

The Rt. Rev. John S. Thornton
Retired Bishop of Idaho
Taucross Farm, Scio, Oregon

PART I

Changes and Chances

Be present, O merciful God, and protect us . . .
so that we who are wearied by the changes and chances of
this life may rest in your eternal changelessness . . .

— from the ancient Service of Compline

CHAPTER ONE

At the Heart of Aging

*Truly I tell you, there are some standing here who
will not taste death until they see that the kingdom
of God has come with power.*

Mark 9:1

At fifteen I set my heart upon learning.
At thirty I established myself in accordance with ritual.
At forty I no longer had perplexities.
At fifty I knew the Mandate of Heaven.
At sixty I was at ease with whatever I heard.
*At seventy I could follow my heart's desire without
transgressing the boundaries of right.*

Confucius

MY FATHER SAID YOU COULD TELL THE STORY
of your life by what happened while you were
here. "I saw the very first automobile come into our
town," he said, "and I saw men walk on the moon. That's
how different the world became in my lifetime." And

how different he became over those years: he started out holding a small god in an ornate box and ended up knowing the vast and universal God. Events shape people, and the oldest generation, over age sixty or so, was shaped by a lifetime of wars: World War II, Korea, Vietnam, Grenada, the Gulf, the cold war, and the war against terrorism. Hiroshima. Nagasaki.

We remember good things, too: the Salk and Sabin vaccines for polio and the end of smallpox. We saw Univac as the miracle of the fifties, and now most of us own personal computers that are enormously faster and more powerful than that "miracle." We were born when radio wasn't too old, and now we have not only color TV but also DVD players and cell phones that do everything except fix breakfast. When I was young I used a huge Speed Graphic camera on my first newspaper job; now I have a little point-and-shoot that takes better pictures as well as a high-resolution scanner whose results I like even better than those of a digital Nikon.

Open the family album and you can look back at yourself as a baby in a snowsuit, a thin child riding a horse, and a scowling teenager; you see yourself graduating from college and maybe holding your children and grandchildren. The greatest gift of your age is also the ability to look back at your spiritual life. In your mental album you can trace the progress you've made in prayer and review the times you thought you'd lost your faith. You can remember when you shook your fist at heaven because a child died or a president was assassinated and when you were so inspired you thought you'd discovered the central secret of life in Christ (until you found the next one). You have probably begun to enjoy some of the changes of older age: the wisdom that comes with maturity, a deeper and more directed prayer life, and a firmer grasp on your relationship with God.

The Difference Death Makes

You may not be so enthusiastic about the fact that age also brings physical limitation and maybe mental or emotional weakness, but even these factors can enhance spirituality rather than impede it. Prayer and spiritual experience at sixty or seventy are not what they were at thirty or fifty. As you age, you pray. And pray differently.

OK, someone says, so what is this spirituality of aging, and how is it really so changed from what came previously? I pray as usual; I've always gone to church and thought about God; I've been praying the rosary or singing in the choir all my life. Is something magically going to change on the day I turn sixty or sixty-five?

Yes. Something will happen. The something that makes a difference is death, and spiritual change begins on the day when, consciously or otherwise, you begin to acknowledge your mortality. The older you get, the more closely that old enemy stalks you and reminds you in a dry, rattling voice that you aren't going to live forever. Sooner or later, the voice insists, you'll leave this world and the people in it—and it may be sooner than later.

Whether you live to be sixty-eight or ninety-five or a hundred fifteen, death is present all the time in the everyday life of an older person, singing its song and shaking its bony finger. And the presence of death means that your prayers are more urgent, your hymn singing more tearful, and your churchgoing shot through with the challenge of letting go of this life and pleading with God for another. Confronting death is the major spiritual exercise of aging. You have to transcend being afraid of the end and arrive at the place where the unmistakable signs of your mortality—including old age's physical or mental breakdowns and the financial surprises that can pop up—determine the liturgies of your old age. Allow yourself to admit that your days are numbered, and God will break through and turn your spirit into the driving force of your life.

Because God is always waiting nearby, like a nervous lover who wants to give you gifts or affection. And when you know you're going to die, God can dive into the new breach in your mind and spirit. And when you sense need, God responds to that need. God can do just so much when you're strong and independent; you don't really feel the lack of God when you're still convinced you're in charge of your life. But because death is inevitable, out of your control, spinning through the universe, and bound to hit you, you have to turn to the One who is running things; and that turn is life changing.

You'll know when that turn comes, perhaps when you say, "Well if I live to see (great-grandchildren, the year 2010, a woman in the White House)." Or when you go to buy trees for your backyard and choose some that are fast growing because you don't have time for those that take twenty years. And one day you discover that although you have plenty to occupy your mind, your spiritual life has become more important. You turn more contemplative, more eager for silence and less interested in external piety. Your mind quiets and quits editing everything. You turn to prayer like a homing pigeon, and some other element of your life that once loomed large now retreats into the background; God has slipped into its place. Every day is an adventure with God, not always pleasant but always exciting, always preparing you for eternal life.

The Turn That Prayer Makes

Most of us who are aging learn to pray constantly. We pray while we're lying awake at night, while taking our prescribed one-mile walk, while waiting in the doctor's office. The nature of our very lives requires that we need more prayer and need it more often. Rather than asking, as younger people sometimes do, "How can I pray more?" we're more likely to ask, "Why would I stay away from prayer?" With death always dangling at the end of the dream, prayer is as necessary as water.

You pray less now about what you want and probably rarely send up the kinds of petitions that you prayed when you were younger. What you longed for at forty either won't do you any good at seventy or you don't want it so much anymore. When you were a young person, you probably begged God for health, guidance, and maybe even wealth or fame. (I remember praying, *God, I don't want to sound materialistic, but . . .*)

And although you're probably faithful with intercessions—anyone our age probably has friends who are gravely ill or even dying and kids and grandkids who are old enough to get in trouble or lose jobs or have dangerous illnesses—your intercessions may not be as directive as they used to be. Now you just bring the person you care for into the circle with you and God, and you stand fast for divine blessing on you and that person. On the other hand, you likely pray a lot more for wisdom. They say there's a direct relationship between grayer hair and the sum total of wisdom, which is a fancy way of saying that old people are wiser. But human wisdom isn't enough; you need divine inspiration to get through the "golden" years and to the end.

A man died in my arms about nine years ago, a man who wasn't old but who had aged considerably during his battle with AIDS. He was a former pastor whose congregation had condemned and deserted him. He had wept for months on the phone to his mother, who wouldn't come to see him. The only visitors he had were Jesus and me, and I couldn't be there all the time. At the moment of his death, he turned to smile at me and said "Thank you," and looked beyond me at someone obviously familiar to him, someone I couldn't see. The man's last words were, "Please, Jesus . . ."

The Suffering We All Endure

Yes. *Please, Jesus! Please, please. Cover my sins and remember not my iniquities. Please, Jesus, undo the times I struck my children or was cold to my spouse or irritable in my classroom. Oh, please, Jesus, forgive the lies I've uttered and the times when I evaded the truth; forgive my greed for everything electronic ever made; forgive my impatience with my mother in her last years.* And I suspect we all want to add, "Please, Jesus, don't let me suffer."

But suffering is part of life, apparently unavoidable and probably necessary and an important part of aging. A crucial moment in the life of the Buddha, Gautama Siddhartha, was the day he ventured outside the gates of his home and encountered three aspects of human life that changed him profoundly: old age, sickness, and death. From then on, he built his spiritual practice with those events always before him. Death ends life on earth, but Buddhists know that the *realization* of death can begin a vigorous spirituality.

Once we thought we were invincible, and then in middle age we became willing to consider our own mortality. The thought of death probably made you tremble for a moment at forty or fifty, but by the time you're about seventy, you become both more fearful and more philosophical. Death is there, yes, but fear has to eventually assent to the end. So when we pray, we beg for grace—the grace to face death without making anyone else miserable, and the grace of a quick departure in our sleep. Nothing long and drawn out and painful.

Because pain allows you to share the sufferings of Christ, even your physical discomfort can become prayer. When arthritis stiffens your joints for a day and makes every movement unbearable, or when a torn rotator cuff shoots agony into your brain, you take part in the overwhelming throes our Savior endured on the cross. A toothache or migraine becomes prayer—hard, difficult prayer to be sure, but nevertheless a spiritual gift because it brings you closer to Christ.

Remember how your grandmother or someone else said, "Offer it up, honey," when you were a child crying with a stomachache or a skinned knee? Don't stop now. The aches and pains of old age don't feel very spiritual, but God ennobles them. When you suffer, keep glancing at Christ on the cross. Perhaps you can't put that prayer into words because you don't completely understand the mystery of suffering. But you do know that pain brings you closer to God. Your sigh of pain places you somewhere at the foot of the cross.

Maybe you're a person who likes to live positively, choosing to ignore death. Of course. We all want to be cheerful and happy, to live in the moment and pretend death isn't there. But that attitude, as Christian as it sounds, can separate you from God. The truth will set you free, Jesus said. You are not free to live on earth forever. To pretend you can is a lie, and a lie is a barrier between you and God. If you tell yourself the truth about death, you are free to live fully, as Christ's joyful, dying creature.

CHAPTER TWO

Learning Death, Choosing Life

*I call heaven and earth to record this day against
you, that I have set before you life and death,
blessing and cursing: therefore choose life.*
Deuteronomy 30:19, KJV

*Live in each season as it passes; breathe the air,
drink the drink, taste the fruit, and resign yourself
to the influences of each.*
Henry David Thoreau

MY FRIEND JEAN CAMPBELL RECENTLY WROTE about the process of her aging, "I'm beginning to hear the applause at the finish line." Because I was once a long-distance runner, I know what she meant. I've won more than one race, and as I ran toward the tape at the end, I'd hear cheering and cries of "Sprint,

sprint!" and clapping, and I gained energy and speed enough to win, just from the sound. As we race through old age and into the rich mystery of death, we need to listen to that applause. Perhaps the cheers are coming from the church triumphant, that community of saints and victors who wait for us in heaven, who hover over our altars at Eucharist, and who encourage us, indeed, toward the finish line.

Learning Death

We spend our lives learning *about* death, but now we have to learn it firsthand. Look back and remember what you can about your earliest awareness of mortality. I first encountered death in the late 1930s, on red soil and rocks that were rich with the presence of God and death. I prayed in the desert at daylight and at night. At dawn, when I first woke, quail and mourning doves echoed my daily guardian angel prayer and the one for copper miners who would flirt that day with the Enemy. Ours was at that time the deepest copper mine in the world, and death lurked around mine openings, thrusting its fluid hands right into the rocks, shaking the supports and tumbling the shafts. My father, who was an engineer and rarely went below the surface, was injured in a cave-in while he was working out the electrical plan at 4,800 feet below ground, and some of my friends' fathers died that day.

Every night I said all the prayers I could remember, including Now I Lay Me Down to Sleep, Gentle Jesus Meek and Mild, and the Our Father. Then I would run through the list of people I wanted God to bless. Since *blessing* was a word that I found abstract, I had come to believe that after I invoked it, God would be unable to smite with death or diseases the persons whom I named—my parents and grandparents and aunts and uncles and cousins—so long as I remembered to pray blessings for them nightly and sign off claiming the name of the Trinity.

I feared that if I forgot to pray for my grandparents or left cousins out of my blessings, God might send upon them vile illness or storms that tore the roofs from their houses. Without my blessings, God could touch them with eternal damnation that ended in a place of fire and devils. I believed this praying to be too great a responsibility for me, and I longed to ask my mother for help in blessing our extended family, but I did not because

Mother, though she was the church organist, was not articulate about religious things. My father listened to my prayers every night. I prayed for his safety and begged God not to let him die, because I suspected that the thread of my own life was attached somehow to his and that if my father were to die, I might also expire, simply curling up like a brown tendril on a sun-devoured vine.

Six weeks after the cave-in that injured my father and took the lives of my friends' fathers, our housekeeper's brother-in-law Alberto, whose wife had left him for another man, sat in a ditch a block from our grammar school and shot himself in the chest. My friend Paul and I discovered him on our way to school. He was still faintly alive, twitching and groaning, with blood smeared over his white shirt and black dress coat. Paul, who was always calm and practical, raced to the school and came back dragging the principal by his hand and a fluttering covey of teachers trailing behind them. The principal ordered us children on to school, but I would not leave immediately. I stood still, resisting the adult hands on my elbows, deliberately memorizing Alberto's face, his black brows that almost met, and his aristocratic nose and jaws bluish with the night's beard. I memorized death, looking at him.

Death danced around us there on the desert, and that death was the root of my spiritual formation. I learned about death long before I understood the Resurrection; men went into the earth and were crushed or died of silicosis of the lung—"rock-in-the-box," the miners called it. Mexican and Native American kids died of tuberculosis. People shot themselves. Nobody explained any of this to me. God and I were alone on all those nights while I struggled in prayer to keep my friends and relatives alive.

Imagining Life after Death

No matter where you learn death, or how or at what time of your life, you have to decide what you think comes after it. Answer this: just what do you think will happen after your death? And how much do you believe whatever that is? Your responses to these questions will shape your spiritual life as you age.

Perhaps the answer depends on what time it is or what mood you're in. Perhaps you wake up in the morning not believing anything; when you die, you're dead, you say. But later—maybe after some coffee and hot oatmeal—you admit that you hope for life after death. Perhaps on Sunday morning, when you have just received Communion, you can sign on to the church's entire teaching about the afterlife.

But what if, when you get there, there's no *there?* What if you don't wake up looking at God, or don't wake up anywhere at all? What if after all those years of prayers and Eucharist celebrations and rosaries and retreats, the whole concept of an afterlife turns out to be something invented by humans?

You'd never know, of course, because if afterlife doesn't exist, then neither does after-death consciousness. But you probably like to flee such thoughts, getting busy with dinner or the lawn or a string of figures. There's no elephant in *your* living room, you tell yourself; you don't have a problem believing in heaven.

But the elephant may be breathing down your neck, and one of these nights when sleep evades you but you're too tired to get up and write or paint a wall or bake cookies, you'll find your mind going back to the subject, over and over. You'll realize that you have to know. You've got to decide whether Jesus really rose from the dead, and you have to decide, probably gasping for breath as you do, whether you will rise also. You have to settle the ultimate questions of faith—as the young woman said in Douglas Adams's *The Hitchhiker's Guide to the Galaxy,* of "God and the Universe and everything."

When I look around at the Christians I know, I wonder if most of them believe in life after death or even in God, because their behavior isn't always consonant with faith; they're busier acquiring treasures in the world than laying up those in heaven. They don't live lives of trust. Few give evidence that they are willing to let God adjudicate any injustices done them but prefer to duke it out on earth. And too few fulfill the words of St. Peter: "even though you do not see him now, you believe in him and rejoice with an indescribable and glorious joy, for you are receiving the outcome of your faith, the salvation of your souls" (1 Peter 1:8–9).

Deciding What You Believe

So now decide once and for all not just whether you believe but whether you will live your life as if you did. You may decide in the middle of a long night, or in a flash as you settle down on the riverbank with your fishing pole, or over a period of time. Sometimes the question of another person—perhaps a child—will help you centralize your faith and choose to believe.

I decided, or rather knew, that I believed in heaven when my four-year-old grandson, Andrew, fought about death—with his friends, his parents, and God. His best friend, Mark, died of cancer, and Andrew was unable to cope with it.

"Kids don't die!" he declared, and we tried and tried to talk with him, but he was adamant. He'd been told that kids didn't die, and now he was in danger himself.

So I took him one day to the Dairy Queen for some ice cream. As I got him in the car and buckled his safety belt he said, "Gra'mother? Wouldn't it be neat if when people died they came alive again?"

"Andrew, somebody did that once," I said as I drove. "Came alive after they died."

"You mean Jesus," Andrew said.

"Yes, Jesus came alive."

After another short burst of silence, he said, "Well, maybe Jesus came alive, but it didn't help Mark. What about Mark and me and Mom and Dad and the baby and the dog and everybody?"

I stopped in the left turn lane and looked into my rearview mirror. I could see his smooth-skinned, blue-eyed face, and he could see me.

"Andrew," I said, "Jesus fixed it so that when we die, we'll all come alive again, too. We call it the Resurrection. Some day, everybody dead will stand up and, well, be alive."

"Really?" His voice was filled with awe. "Everybody? Do you mean alive, or just sort of in heaven like a ghost or something?"

"No, I mean alive," I said, parking in front of the Dairy Queen. I unbuckled my seat belt and was starting to get out when Andrew's voice caught my heart and broke it.

"Gra'mother?" he said, small and quiet. "Gra'mother, is this like Santa Claus?"

I was frozen with terror. "What do you mean, like Santa Claus?"

"You know. A story you tell little kids."

Sweat beaded up on my forehead and upper lip, sweat like clots of blood. My faith was on its mettle now. *Was* the Resurrection story like Santa Claus, like the tooth fairy, a story you tell gullible little kids? Did I tell the Jesus legend as a salve to sweeten reality, to perfume the hopeless air of death and corruption? I gasped for breath and said, "I know that my redeemer liveth."

"What?" Andrew said.

"And that he shall stand in the latter day upon the earth," I said.

"*What?*"

"And though worms destroy this body, yet in my flesh shall I see God," I said, louder and clearer, my heart thrumming.

The sun and moon, motionless above us, brightened the dashboard of my car until my eyes watered. I leaped from the car and opened the back door. My fingers flew over Andrew's seat belt and I grabbed him up in my arms, long and heavy, since he was nearly five, and I cried, "No, Andrew, it's not like Santa Claus. It's true and I believe it. We'll all come alive again."

The light had grown so great that I searched the sky for a comet or fireball or Christ returning. I set Andrew's feet on the parking-lot asphalt.

"It's true." I said. "Jesus will come back and we'll all be alive again and live forever."

It was late winter, but light pummeled at the trees until I was sure they had budded. The air was rife with the fragrance of life, real life on earth.

And we went inside and ate all the ice cream in the world. It was a party where Andrew was the host and Christ the honored guest, a party attended by angels.

On that day, I decided to believe without antago-
nism, to take God at God's word. Sure, questions still
pop into my mind, especially in the darkness of early
winter mornings when every joint in my body is
inflamed and I wonder if I can even get up. But I don't
fight God about the truth now, don't order God to
answer my questions or to give me a sign if indeed God
is listening. I chose faith over despair, life over death, and
reason over the insanity of unbelief.

Wagering on God's Word

People need to see faith in action. Suicide bombers are
wrong in what they do, but they demonstrate genuine faith.
People don't strap plastic explosives to themselves and go to
a bank or mall and blow themselves up if they don't believe
that God is waiting for them, that Paradise is guaranteed.

If you can't bear to think of the words *terrorists* and
faith in the same sentence, then consider the saints who
were burned to death or eaten by lions or beheaded for
their belief in Christ. Consider the Roman martyrs who
entered the Colosseum singing. Or St. Thomas More,
who thanked his executioner for sending him to God. Or
the convict who went to the electric chair saying "I'll see

you in the Morning." Could you hold on that completely to God's promises? Can you maintain the belief that you'll awake resurrected, perfected, and glorified?

You open either the door to heaven or the door to disbelief. You don't have to have a mystical experience or be swept into faith; just choose to believe in God, in the sacrifice of Christ, and begin to live your life that way. You can even take the bet made by the seventeenth-century French mathematician Blaise Pascal. He was unimpressed by any elaborate mathematical or philosophical calculus for the probability for God's existence. Instead, he wagered that God existed and made a decision to believe and live in accordance with God's rules.

"If at the end of my life I've been wrong," he said, "I have lost nothing. But if I am right, I have gained everything." He chose faith over floundering around in the swamp of uncertainty. And having chosen faith, Pascal became a great Christian but without fanfare. In fact, it is only because he sewed a parchment memorial of the event inside his coat pocket that history knows of the most important spiritual event in his life—the "Night of Fire" on November 23, 1654, when for about two hours he was overwhelmed by tears of joy. The impersonal deism of philosophers no longer worked, and the true God revealed godself to him.

"Fire," Pascal wrote later. "The God of Abraham, the God of Isaac, the God of Jacob. Not of the philosophers and intellectuals. . . . The God of Jesus Christ . . . joy, joy, joy . . ."

By coming to Christ, you can, like Pascal, come to yourself in a new and powerful way. He wrote in his *Pensées,* "Not only do we only know God through Jesus Christ, but we only know ourselves through Jesus Christ; we only know life and death through Jesus Christ. Apart from Jesus Christ we cannot know the meaning of our life or of our death, of God, or of ourselves." Can you ask for more than this?

So how do you settle once and for all your questions about whether God is legitimate, whether Jesus Christ really rose from the dead, and finally, whether you will really rise from the dead? How? Pray. Confess. (Maybe everyone over sixty should make a Good Act of Contrition once an hour.) Entreat Christ to be part of your old age: *Christ, come and walk with me through my old age. Be in my mouth when I speak to those who are younger; be my vision and hearing even when mine are failing, so that what I perceive is truth, your truth. And above all, stand*

between the Throne and my sins and take me to heaven when
death overtakes me.

Inviting God In

Salvation isn't a matter of morality or virtue; it's a question of holiness, of living a redeemed and sacred life. Although the English-speaking world is almost incurably Pelagian and we practically elbow God out of the way in our efforts to save ourselves, trying to be good won't ever be good enough. Goodness is a function of holiness, not the root of it. Holiness comes from actively allowing God to tinker with your soul. Oddly enough, older age—when you most need God's work in your life—is the time when you might find it hardest to allow God in. You've been a grownup for a long time, and becoming like a little child sounds simple but is quite complicated.

I want grace to fall on me, not wait on my doorstep to be invited in.

"I don't know why you're saying this. You know you're loved and forgiven," says a friend who believes that "once saved, always saved."

Do I know? That woman is in her early forties, probably not old enough yet to know that in coming years faith in the midst of pain and worry will be a struggle, or that her main emotions toward God can be anger or fear. She probably doesn't wonder yet if the salvation she grabbed during her teens was really long-lasting enough to keep her in the kingdom. But I do. Am I redeemed? Do I have unconfessed sins that could send me to hell?

If I ran the kingdom, if I were God, I wouldn't make people go through aging or death or purgatory. The God I'd like would be a cross between a fairy godmother and Santa Claus with maybe a little bit of an innocuous Jesus thrown in. I'd make everybody happy all the time, let them be healthy to, say, one hundred years of age, and then snatch them to heaven quickly without the terrifying process of physical death. But since I am not the deity, I have a mysterious, invisible God who allows me to suffer on earth. Having been given enough of that situation, including the physical discomfort and financial worries of aging, I sometimes want to shake my fist at heaven. Or worse yet, just walk away from God altogether.

It's no accident then that the deadliest sin of older age is acedia, the sin of spiritual torpor that is sometimes badly called sloth; the sin is not physical laziness but a kind of slow murder of the spirit. The answer is always prayer—but that's the one thing you can't make yourself do when you're slothful. A theologian once described the state as "the day you'd be cynical about everything, if you had the energy." But this isn't the cynicism of youth; this rises out of the anger of old age, anger that God is doing this to you, allowing it to happen, or not being involved in it, depending on your theology.

Rage underlies a lot of illnesses and a lot of the sputtering, short-circuited emotion associated with aging. And rage leads to sloth, then sloth to loss of faith. Prayer is the only way out, but prayer comes hard to the slothful, to the old, to those struggling for faith. Sometimes their prayer is only, "God, let it all be true," which is an unreasonable prayer, because if it isn't all true, then who are they praying to? So to stay out of the sloth trap, here is what you have to do: tend the faith you've chosen, and stay in touch with your own spirit and with God.

How will you know that Jesus Christ has responded to your invitation to share your old age? Will you suddenly become immune to the threats of stroke or adult-onset diabetes or leukemia? If God smiles on you, will you be strong and independent and full of energy? Will money appear from nowhere to pay off charge cards or buy expensive prescriptions? Will your roof sprout new shingles or your lawn stay weed free because Christ says "Yes" to your cry for his presence?

Well, of course not. Even the greatest of the saints had diseases and problems, and their nerves were sometimes on edge. The desert fathers were attacked by visions of impure women and great spreads of food; some saints had stigmata that bled until they were anemic. What Christ's operation in human life does provide us with is courage and grace with moments of ineffable joy and, even in the darkness, the promise of light. Christ's operation within us never carries the guarantee that we will be healthy or rich or even happy. The guarantee is that we are redeemed.

So you have two choices: you can either view all this as a mystery to be lived out or as a problem that must be understood and solved. Some days I'm content with mystery and other days I *have* to get an answer. But regardless of which choice I make, I know that God is somewhere in the center of this, that neither the mystery nor the answer will make any sense without the saving grace of Jesus Christ, and that the situation will ultimately bring me to my knees.

Moses summoned all Israel and said to them: "Therefore choose life." He was sending them into the Promised Land, where he could not go, and he laid life and death before them, offering them blessings or curses. "Therefore choose life," he said, "loving the Lord your God, obeying him, and holding fast to him; for that means life to you."

Choose. Choose to believe, and when doubts rise again, remind yourself of the day and hour when you decided that your future was in God's hands. Then celebrate your choice. This is critical. No, it is absolutely essential that you tell yourself, and God, once and for all, that you believe Jesus rose from the dead.

And that you, too, will rise, and not just be sort of in heaven like a ghost or something.

CHAPTER THREE

Prayer and the Aging Process

Do not cast me off in the time of old age; do not forsake me when my strength is spent.

Psalm 71:9

Last Chance Farm

Sign in southern New Jersey

NEXT TO DEATH, THE GREATEST FEAR IN old age is old age. You're afraid you'll become like the people you've seen in nursing homes, the ones who come by taxi or group van to church. They ride in wheelchairs or lean on their walkers, their identities concealed within failing bodies. And you don't want to be among them. They shuffle when they walk, their skin is ragged and blotched, their eyes are red rimmed and vacant, and you swear you'll never look like that, ever.

Changes in the Body

But you *may* look like that, no matter how many emollients you rub into your hands and face and no matter how many exercise classes you attend. Your face may blossom with brown age spots and Grand Canyon wrinkles; perhaps your skin will thin until your arms and legs are spattered with dark purple hematomas. You may become old and doddering and talk so slowly that you make people impatient. In old age you might limp and falter with arthritic knees or your backbone could take on a 90-degree angle. You might have to ask other people to open your jars or reach for things overhead. Putting on a pair of shoes may become a major task, and if you're a woman, the challenges of donning a pair of pantyhose could make you late to church. Perhaps eventually you will walk like a penguin, holding your spouse's hand—which people will think is "cute"—not for affection but because you both fear falling.

So you pray a lot as you age. You pray not to feel ugly and to be a beacon, not a burden, to your family or friends. You pray that God will take you before people nod and sigh and say things like "Wouldn't it be a blessing if she'd go?" You pray that if your old age must be colored by Parkinson's disease or crippling arthritis, you'll maintain grace and kindness instead of becoming self-centered and mean spirited.

Often you'll pray because you're uncomfortable. Unless you're lucky or a lifelong athlete, your aging body can remind you that more of your years are behind you than ahead of you and that while you're writing out a will and taking vitamin E and eating blueberries to keep your memory strong, you need a giant dollop of prayer. You pray to enter oldest age with grace and to be spared the worst and most humiliating disabilities.

"I'm not moving to Sun City," my Uncle Fred used to say in his early seventies, in spite of the fact that Aunt Betty wanted to live in a retirement community there. "I don't play golf, and I don't want to talk about my bowels." Some of us feel betrayed by our human plumbing and pipes; either our inward parts have pinched together so that no amount of cereal or salad makes anything happen, or we're overwhelmed with urgency caused by irritable bowel syndrome. Chances are, whatever goes wrong will go wrong either with the brain—a paralyzing stroke or dementia—or below the waist: a kidney stone, a blocked intestine, a urinary tract infection, a prostate or ovarian disorder. The diuretics we take for high blood pressure or congestion make us pee all the time, sometimes when we sneeze in polite company. Our ailments bring us to doctors' offices and hospitals, where unspeakable indignities are performed upon us. Uncle Fred ended his life having to talk a lot about his bowels because his fatal illness was colon cancer.

Even if you're not sick, age can bring you some special humiliations. A few days ago I attended a meeting, then stopped at the market to pick up a few things. I looked good: I'd gone to some trouble with my face and hair, and I had on my best black suit and a ruby bracelet that swung back and forth on my wrist as I pushed my cart around.

A young woman, also pushing a cart, was screaming at her five children and smacking them, and I looked at her. Usually a look is all it takes to make harried mothers realize how they appear and sound. But this woman glared back and hollered, "Don't look at me, you old fart."

I almost checked to see if some elderly hag was behind me. Surely, she didn't mean *me*, with my suit and my sleek ash-blond pageboy and my silver earrings, did she?

Yes, she did. Her anger saw through all those trappings and identified me as what I really was: an aging woman who wasn't exactly minding her own business.

But the second half of her epithet threw me into a class I'd never felt I belonged in, and it stung. Old *fart?* Ugly, disgusting, stupid, worthless, offensive throwaway woman? I didn't know whether to laugh or cry; but for several days I was bemused by the experience.

I don't know why God doesn't design us to become more appealing in old age. Autumn trees are beautiful, but human beings rarely become more physically attractive as they get older. But if we always loved our faces and bodies, would we ever be willing to leave them? I think the changes in appearance are part of the plan. Just as adolescent girls hate their mothers for a while and thus are better able emotionally to leave home, we get ready for a spiritual body by hating this one. And the assignment God gives us isn't to look young forever or to lead a jolly life: God wants us to give meaning to the time we're on earth.

A Change of Clothing

Your clothing has to change in old age: you need to weave a festal garment so you don't get caught underdressed at the wedding feast and thrown into outer darkness, like the guests in the Matthew 22 parable. Your autumn is a time for putting on not external but *eternal* splendor, to clothe yourself with spiritual beauty.

Getting ready for heaven isn't just a matter of being good, of compiling a list of rules to follow so that if you drop dead without asking for forgiveness you won't plunge into hell for your latest series of sins. If preparing to meet God were that easy, you'd probably live in a highly moral society where people were scared to death of God and governed themselves accordingly. But that isn't how it works: morality springs from spiritual life but can't replace it. The task at hand is to become holy, to let fire like Pascal's heat your old age and dying and become a cloak of spiritual fire; that fire is available only through earnest, concentrated prayer and adoration.

Now is the time to make prayer the day's priority, to develop a rich spiritual practice, to transform ordinary time. If you're not in the habit of centering prayer or meditation or silence, don't expect it to come easily. Start today, and maybe in a hundred years you'll be satisfied that you have the attention you need to stay with it. You're not alone. John Donne said in the seventeenth century, "A memory of yesterday's pleasures, a fear of tomorrow's dangers, a straw under my knees, a noise in my ear, a light in my eye, an anything, a nothing, a fancy, a chimera in my brain, troubles me in my prayers."

Nevertheless, strive and strive and strive, as St. Teresa of Ávila said somewhere. Make your old age a time of growing closer, closer to God. The Sufi writer Ibn al-'Arabi believed in a personal relationship with God, a private, intimate dialogue between an individual and his Lord. He said, "Do everything you do in order to come close to your Lord in your worship and prayers. Think that each deed may be your last act, each prayer your last prostration, that you may not have another chance."

In this same spirit I was struck once by a sign over the priest's vesting table in a church sacristy that read, "Remember, O Priest, that this is your first Communion, your last Communion, your only Communion." So if you don't like the idea that each deed might be your last, imagine that the act will be your only one. One chance for mercy or compassion or generosity of spirit, one opportunity to make a difference in the world. With every new line in your face should come a new way of meditating. Use the hours you might spend watching a video to do some spiritual reading instead, maybe delving back into the old

Christian classics (for more information on these titles and authors see the Suggested Reading section beginning on page 275): *The Imitation of Christ, The Interior Castle, Revelations of Divine Love, Mere Christianity,* and *The Practice of the Presence of God.* Read William McNamara and Evelyn Underhill. Read Rabbi Abraham Heschel's writings and those of Sister Macrina Wiederkehr and Sister Joan Chittister. If you've read all those books, read them again, this time applying everything they say to aging. For instance, when Thomas à Kempis says in the opening section of *The Imitation of Christ,* "'He who follows Me, walks not in darkness,' says the Lord," think of following Christ through the next five or ten or twenty years, into old age and even possible suffering. And think about your attitude toward aging when St. Teresa of Ávila says, "It is really a perfect misery to be alive when we have always to be going about like men with enemies at their gates, who cannot lay aside their arms even when sleeping or eating, and are always afraid of being surprised by a breaching of their fortress in some weak spot." Hoo, boy. Do you consider age to be the breaching of your strong will? And as a result, are you heading into perfect misery? Well, look for hope in C. S. Lewis, who says, "If

I find in myself a desire which no experience in this world can satisfy, the most probable explanation is that I was made for another world." Can anything better describe the process at the end of your time?

A New Concentration on Scripture

Of course, you can turn to the Bible in what might be a new way. You may have practiced lectio divina all your life, or you may have no idea what it is. "Lectio," as it is most commonly called, is a way toward awareness of God's presence through a four-step process: lectio is receiving the word of God, meditatio is allowing the Word to be present within you, oratio is prayer, and contemplatio is resting in the presence of God. You can pick Scriptures and work with them until they become part of you—and part of your old age.

Begin by reading a passage of Scripture (you can find several appropriate ones in the Scriptures section at the back of this book). St. Benedict encouraged his followers to "hear with the heart." Few of his monks could read, and those who could didn't own their own Bibles in that time before the printing press; so the Word was read aloud during mealtimes and in the chapel. But you can invest yourself every day by reading a short passage of Scripture; then let the words become what Teresa called "mental prayer." Apply the words to your own life and your aging. Then pray the words. For instance, when you read from Psalm 18:46, "The Lord lives! Blessed be my rock, / and exalted be the God of my salvation," say these words back to God: *Thank you, God, for your life inside me . . . You are the rock who carries me to safety and my salvation even when I can no longer do for myself . . .* And finally, sit for at least ten minutes in absolute silence, letting the words of Scripture dance and sing within you even when you are not concentrating.

Lectio can call up what's buried inside you, and your prayers can have new richness and fervor when you use this spiritual device every day. Tend your faith. Pray without ceasing, bless God every moment, and constantly inhale the name of God. Make Eucharist every day if you can, so that Christ's body will sustain your aging physical self. Read the Bible, asking God to set fire to the words in your heart. Meditate every day to seek the calm joy of God. And set your face toward heaven the same way Jesus set his toward Jerusalem. Ask that

God use the suffering part of aging to let you share the sufferings of Christ. Affirm once more that you believe in the resurrection of the dead and the life everlasting and that when you doubt it, you'll firmly set your foot back on the path of belief. And pray diligently that you might keep this belief until the morning when you open your eyes, looking into the face of the Son of God.

CHAPTER FOUR

Losses

Even to your old age I am [God],
even when you turn gray I will carry you.

Isaiah 46:4

There's no such thing as old age;
there is only sorrow.

Edith Wharton

BOUT A YEAR AGO, A FRIEND OF MINE WAS
speaking bitterly of loss. Although the fall day was
bright—a rarity here in the Pacific Northwest—with
lavender crocuses and dark chrysanthemums blooming,
and autumn leaves blazing scarlet and saffron, our little
group was morose, walking slowly through manicured
lawns. We had been to the funeral of a good friend, too
young to die, and now we were at the cemetery to attend
the interment. Afterward one of the men in our group
said, "I can't stand all this losing! Half my friends are dead

or dying. My parents are gone and so is one of my brothers. I've been forced into retirement, so I've lost my job. I've lost my close-up vision. I'm losing my hair and my teeth are going fast. My car was burgled last week, so I've lost my radio and my cell phone. And I had to have my dog put to sleep. What more does God want from me?"

I didn't try to answer him then—he was in too bad a mood for a philosophical discussion, and besides, we had to drive to the funeral reception—but his words kept repeating themselves in my mind. I looked around at my own life and started counting my losses. I've lost both parents, too, and several friends have succumbed to heart attacks and cancer and strokes. Like that of my friend's, my eyesight is not wonderful: I now have three pairs of glasses for different occupations, and my close-up vision requires total correction. I'm losing the hearing in my left ear. The color in my blond-streaked brown hair is phony—I've lost the real pigment. And the worst fear I have—like that of many people over sixty-five—isn't cancer, it's loss of my wits. Will I be taken down with some kind of dementia or lose my independence and live in a nursing home, drooling and fighting the nurses?

I originally started this chapter shortly before the terrorist attacks on the World Trade Center and the

Pentagon and the plane crash in Pennsylvania. But I might well have written it afterward, because after that day, the country's perception of loss changed forever. The loss of life, to say nothing of the collapse and disappearance of an important landmark, was massive, and the shock of loss soon gave rise to national grief and mourning. Loss meant a pile of bodies and rubble in the World Trade Center plaza. Loss was a brave man on a plane who asked an operator to pray the Our Father with him. Loss suggested a failure in our national intelligence network and the shock of this realization to every citizen. People who had never experienced personal loss suddenly found themselves bereft, and the whole country began to mourn not just for the dead, but for the sense of safety that had always characterized America.

When land mines rob people of limbs and lives or war deprives them of food, shelter, or even bodily safety—even when individual loss is by those standards trivial—it can feel unbearable. Pile up even the smallest losses along with the big ones, and the sense of deprivation can be, as it was for my friend at the cemetery, overwhelming. And as you journey into old age, you're surrounded by reductions in friendships and intimate relationships. Your faithful, elderly dog dies—or worse yet, you have to have her put to sleep. Your body suffers many large and small disasters. Your finances may be in dire jeopardy; many of us at retirement lose a good portion of our income. To add to the discomfiture of small losses, it's also harder to be old because eyesight problems and stiffness of limbs can make it difficult even to look for the little things we've dropped or misplaced.

Turning to God in Our Loss

A lost earring or a pair of glasses is certainly nothing compared to the death of a friend, or worse, a husband or wife. If the individual has gone through months of coma or chemotherapy or dementia, your loss began long before the moment of death. You may have started saying goodbye months earlier—or you may have withheld your grief, believing that a miracle would happen and that your loved one would be restored. And since miracles apparently do sometimes happen, your "denial" was not, in the Christian view at any rate, unrealistic.

But if your loss was sudden, if your husband or wife or sibling went to work or to play golf or to fish at a trout farm, and later you got word from the authorities of that person's death, you didn't even have time to think about losing him or her, much less get a chance to say goodbye. Shock can delay personal grief, and taking care of funeral arrangements and legalities may postpone your real mourning for a while.

Yet in the midst of your shock and busyness, you can pray. Jesus promised that those who mourn would be comforted. So as quickly as possible, engage your grief and work it through—not just so you can resolve it, but so you can let God flow into the empty places of your life. Because unlike my friend at the cemetery, I think I know what God wants from us: everything.

Sometimes loss is easier when we share it with hundreds of others, as after an earthquake or hurricane. The destruction on September 11, 2001, brought people together the way my own neighborhood came together when a young boy with an assault rifle murdered his parents, then went to the local high school and began gunning down the students. Three died, one was permanently brain damaged, and some still live in wheelchairs. After that shooting, which was on CNN within an hour, we stood in little clumps in the supermarket parking lot; people who had never met or spoken to one another were now talking and expressing shock. We filled the local churches, held hands, and prayed steadily.

That certainly isn't to say that God is killing our friends in order to get our attention. God would not wipe out innocent members of the human race or our pets or our jobs just to make us dependent. The epistle of James says, "No one, when tempted [or tested], should say 'I am being tempted by God'; for God cannot be tempted by evil and he himself tempts no one. . . . Every generous act of giving, with every perfect gift, is from above, coming down from the Father of lights, with whom there is no variation or shadow due to change" (1:13–17).

God isn't cruel or capricious; our losses are due to the "normal" process of aging and to our living in an imperfect world. But God is making a demand on our attention, not taking things away from us but whispering, "Mourn your loss, but I will fill the gap that person left in your life. I'll be your mother and your friend and your lost youth."

Of course, like a scared little boy who tells his mother that God isn't enough in the dark and that he needs something with skin on it, we want something more visible than God. And there are even people who refuse God's presence, angry at the inevitable and concentrating on what they've lost rather than what they can bring to the world.

I know a man—I'll call him Chuck—who has been grousing for more than thirty years because his son-in-law, a stock broker, lost Chuck's $50,000 by investing it in a mutual fund that went belly up in the 1970s.

"I thought I'd make my old age secure by tripling my money," he said. "Now I have to live on my retirement payments and Social Security." Actually, his retirement offers him a comfortable living; he left his job as an officer of a company. His house is paid off, and despite that one big market loss, he still has a sizable portion of his savings and inheritance and is earning money with blue-chip stocks—which the son-in-law also chose for him. Chuck and his longtime faithful wife are very comfortable; but he's lugging heavy "loss" baggage through life. Instead of turning to God in thanksgiving for what he has, he's replaced worship with regret and sadness. And at seventy-six, he's still unpleasant to his fifty-three-year-old son-in-law, thereby alienating his daughter and grandkids. He hasn't turned to God; he prefers anger and resentment to getting fit for heaven.

Then there's Claire. She's already had a lot of losses: her parents were killed when she was twenty-two, and she had no brothers or sisters. Her philandering husband left her on her fortieth birthday and has married three times since. Claire got a divorce and a church annulment and thought she had put all her losses behind her. But the catastrophe she can't or won't recover from is the loss of the man she met when she was fifty. He was dashing, handsome, and gave her an engagement ring. Then, a few weeks before their planned nuptials, the man took off, using one of Claire's credit cards to finance his escape and cleaning out her bank account. That was twenty years ago, and Claire still weeps when she talks about it. She's chosen regret over love for God.

Life and death are a pilgrimage, and at the end of that pilgrimage is God, face to face. So why are we so concerned about earthly loss and so unwilling to revel in earthly joy? Most of us don't spend a whole lifetime grieving our losses. But sometimes we bury our feelings and they fester, or we spend too much time thinking about what we don't have and guarding what we might lose, instead of filling ourselves with the presence of God. No emptiness or lack or loss could be so great as the loss of God's presence in our lives.

Letting Go of Big and Little Things

Psychologists say that people often find their identities in their belongings. The advanced pack rat—whose home and garage are stuffed with broken typewriters, stacks of old magazines, thirty years' accumulation of clothes, broken crockery that's been waiting eons to be mended, and many boxes of miscellaneous accumulations—would, if deprived of all that, very likely feel as if he or she had also lost personhood. Most of us aren't that extreme, either in our collecting or in how much value we place on our possessions. But we do feel as if some part of our personality can be lost when something or someone important to us dies or is destroyed or lost. And when it's part of our body or a physical function—our hair, our teeth, our sexual potency, or an organ—we need to consciously grieve the loss.

We don't look to God and ignore the loss; we look to God as we grieve the loss, and *then* we let God fill the gap. If you try to shrug off defeat or destruction, pretending to be serene and unhurt while inwardly suffering, or worse, quenching and stuffing your feelings into your unconscious, you'll never be able to invite God to occupy your heart. That heart will already be full of unrecognized regret and grief.

The first stage of grief, in the Kübler-Ross paradigm, is denial, and the last, acceptance. Perhaps a better way to express acceptance, when it concerns the losses in life, is coming to a sense of letting go, a state that Jean-Pierre de Caussade, a Jesuit spiritual writer of the sixteenth century, described as "complete and utter abandonment to the will of God."

So it all comes back to God again? Yes, but by way of the letting-go process that first assumes that God will mercifully heal your sense of deprivation. You have to believe that God is for you and wants good in your life. Then you take yourself through the phases of mourning.

I think grief dissipates more easily if you journal your experience. Even if you've never been a journal writer and you don't really want to record what happens and what you think for the rest of your life, try doing so as you mend your sense of loss. You may have to reach back into your youth to find all the unresolved misfortunes that took something or somebody away from you, but then allow yourself to process your feelings, to get in touch with anger and depression. You may find yourself trying to rewrite history so that things turn out differently in your memory, which is a form of the bargaining that grief counselors talk about. You know what happened, but you imagine scenes in which you save the business or the friendship or the marriage, or in which you find whatever it is you lost.

Esther Armstrong and Dale Stitt, editors of the spirituality newsletter *Journey into Freedom,* say in the July 1998 issue, "While letting go could be the greatest gift we can give God, ourselves, and others, it is also, without doubt, one of the most difficult and painful spiritual disciplines. The pain of letting go sometimes seems so unbearable that it is easy to understand why we often put up walls of protection around ourselves, why we enter into unproductive and destructive patterns of behavior."

If letting go is so painful, why does God ask us to do it? Why has every great spiritual leader from Jesus to Gandhi told us to let go, give up, put our minds on what is above, and shed our worldly goods? Why did Jesus say to the virtuous, rich young man in the book of Matthew, "If you wish to be perfect, go, sell your possessions, and give the money to the poor, and you will have treasure in heaven; then come, follow me" (19:21)?

Why? Because, as Jesus says earlier in Matthew, where your treasure is, there your heart will be also. The rich young man's possessions kept his heart on earthly things. Are you able to walk away from your possessions to follow the Master? Imagine Jesus saying to you, "Let go of all your old losses and give your energy to doing good, and you will have treasure in heaven; then come, follow me."

Once you have mourned your losses, don't create a cemetery for them in your heart. Instead, offer them up to God, and *let go*. Letting go means wiping the slate clean. If someone abandoned you, forgive him and ask God to forgive him. If someone close to you died, mourn her properly and then treasure her memory, thanking God for the time you had together. If you lost money or possessions, give them to God; with God looking after them, you don't have to worry about finding them or getting them back. If you even remember that someone borrowed a book from you two years ago, let go of it. You may never get it back, but it's not worth what a grudge can do to you.

We are affected physically when we don't let go. Worrying or holding grudges or hanging on to grief can send you into depression, which will cause your system to overproduce cortisone, thus lowering your immune system. Not only will you be more prone to catch cold, but your weakened immune system could give rise to pneumonia, shingles, and a host of other serious problems.

We are affected emotionally when we don't let go. Letting go will relieve you of acute or chronic anxiety and depression and make you more available as a wise friend and counselor. Having divested yourself of everything you've lost and having handed what you still own over to God, you're free and untrammeled, able to think and do what you want for a change.

And your spirit can soar when you come to terms with loss and entrust your life to God completely, abandoning your will, as the writer de Caussade insists. The minute you let go of even a tiny loss, you'll feel relieved; imagine what total relinquishment can do for you.

Giving Thanks

There's a final step in the process of accepting your losses, a step Kübler-Ross doesn't list because it's a totally spiritual experience. After you've surrendered your deprivation to God and let go of whatever you've lost, the end is thanksgiving, and it has three phases. The first phase is thanking God that you had the relationship or the belonging in the first place, something we often forget to do.

Recently a friend of mine e-mailed that her sister was close to death and asked for my prayers. I wrote back in sympathy, adding that I wish I'd ever had a sister to pray for. To my astonishment, the friend called me in tears, saying that after she read my e-mail, she realized she'd never thanked God for the fifty years she and her sister had enjoyed together. To let go of someone or something you've loved doesn't mean you quit caring. Thank God for what you had.

Then take the second step, that of thanking God for the opportunity to heal your memories and start living again. Be grateful that anger fades, that you can forget your injuries and, instead of writhing in pain, you can bask in God's forgiveness and restoration.

And finally, look for signs around you that remind you of the promise ahead. Whatever sign you find to remind you that everything will be resurrected, whether it be goldfinches or butterflies or Easter morning, thank

God for filling the emptiness your loss left in you. Turn your thanks into praise; like the Psalms, laud God for being majestic and powerful and beautiful. Because in the end, it will be God, not someone or something you lost, who whispers "Welcome home" when you finally get to heaven.

CHAPTER FIVE

Turn Back

It is sown a physical body, it is raised a spiritual
body. If there is a physical body, there is also a
spiritual body. Thus it is written, "The first man,
Adam, became a living being"; the last Adam
became a life-giving spirit.
1 Corinthians 15:44–45

SHIRLEY VALENTINE, THE MOVIE HEROINE WHO talked to her kitchen wall because she felt trapped, defined what an unhealthy old age can become. "Most of us die . . . long before we're dead," she said. "And what kills us is the terrible weight of all this unused life that we carry around." Plenty of "unused life" probably lies inside each of us. The human mind and body are designed to live in rhythm, where both mind and body need to be nourished and rebuilt and energized.

Why do I exist in a physical body? Why did God make me? And how am I supposed to care for the clay of my body and the pneuma that occupies it? I don't want a catechetical answer, one that says I was created to love and serve. No, I demand to know just what God had in mind.

Part of the answer must be that God creates matter and likes it; God creates galaxies, quasars, planets, moons, asteroids, ice, snow, and blazing sunshine and calls it good. We are the *adam* (human) from the *adama*, the soil or clay. We are incarnate, and ours is an incarnational God who made us, body and soul.

Balance between Body and Soul

When I read *Prevention* magazine, I resolve to take brisk walks, eat great platters full of vegetables, and drink gallons of green tea. But when I search the Bible, I find the writer of Ecclesiastes saying, "Go, eat your bread with enjoyment, and drink your wine with a merry heart; for God has long ago approved what you do" (9:7). Well, somewhere between *Prevention*'s urging and the glib assertion of Ecclesiastes lies the balance. Rhythm is the name of the game where mental and physical health are concerned, and God designed two great concepts to keep that cycle going: Shabbat and shalom.

We're supposed to do two things on Shabbat, or Sabbath: rest and reflect on the nature of God. We no longer enjoy the Jewish Sabbath customs, but we're still commanded to rest in God. I get tired just looking at the way some people spend their weekends, water- or snow skiing, traveling fifty miles each way pulling a boat trailer or a herd of snowmobiles. Some people don't even seek recreation much; they take their work home with them every day and hammer away on their laptops. I see mothers rushing home from church to do five loads of wash and cook for the next week, and I wonder if they ever really rest. Rest is vital and you may have to teach yourself to do it. Start by imagining life without rest; imagine working seven days a week with no time off for refreshment or recreation. Imagine living without sleep.

On the other hand, life without action and work isn't advisable, either. Lack of movement causes your bones to thin, your muscles to atrophy, and your mind to break down. No movement also means no risk, and no risk means you have abandoned the spirit of youth and settled in, the way a house settles on a lot with too much ground fill. Being able to move, to dance, to go places, and to take risks is a major way to slow at least the psychological aging process, but you also have to do something about your body. And if for some reason you're no longer able to move your physical form, move your mind and keep the spirit of adventure alive.

Shalom means more than peace: shalom is peace plus harmony and balance. The Navajo prayers that end *In beauty it is finished* call up shalom. You must have shalom at your center and Shabbat at the end of your work. Peace as you labor, then peace as you rest. That's the pattern God showed us on the mountain of the Presence.

Shalom is a country where you can live in peace, and when you dwell in shalom, the aging process might gray your hair and wear your knees out, but it can't touch the delighted and joyful man or woman inside, the person who knows God intimately and knows that in beauty all things are finished. You can have peace not as the world gives—the peace of Christ is nothing like the relaxation you get from a martini or a massage—and that passes all understanding. Peace that may not even make sense when the rest of the world has apparently gone mad; peace based on trust.

When you trust God with your life, and I mean every second of your life, you have absolute shalom. Until you achieve peace of heart and soul, losing ten pounds and keeping it off won't matter, and neither will keeping the wrinkles off your cheeks. If you're stressed out and unhappy with your job or your domestic situation—or your old age—your face will show it and your body will act it out by exaggerating the jabs of arthritis or the choking of heartburn. Your blood pressure can shoot up and you can't eat or sleep well if you don't have peace at the center of your life.

But Christians take better care of their immortal souls than we do the temples that enclose them, and we can fall into the false belief that we are low and evil by nature, snaky and not worth kicking into hell. I have a real problem with that. If we are so awful, why does God bother with us? If the lowest life form is more pleasing to God than humanity, then why was Christ crucified? An interviewer once asked the writer Annie Dillard whether she didn't think that we are depraved and disgusting and an offense to God, and she answered, "Well, we were good enough to deserve the Incarnation, weren't we?"

I think we have to look at the physical body as more than a temporary enclosure for the spirit. Although St. Paul spoke with derision about his animal body, and St. Francis referred to his corporal self as "Brother Ass," Jesus gave us the sacrament of Communion by saying, "This is my body." And we say in the Nicene Creed that we believe in the resurrection of the body, that we'll be raised as Christ was raised, that the body is part of immortality. Even in the Old Testament, Job said, "For I know that my Redeemer lives, / and that at the last he will stand upon the earth; and after my skin has been thus destroyed, / then in my flesh I shall see God" (19:25–26). The body is part of God's package, so just as I prepare my soul for life hereafter, I have to prepare my body for resurrection. The body is not, says Father Thomas Ryan, the soul's prison; it, too, is created by God and destined for resurrection. His books on meditation, Christian yoga, and mental discipline all stress the importance of considering the body and spirit a single object.

People who want to reverse, or at least slow, the process of old age, have to be at peace with their world and their own conscience. They need to get enough rest, eat what God deems best, and move the body. That's the whole prescription from heaven, where our bodies were designed. At our age, we need a lot less fat and a lot more fresh fruits and vegetables. That's it. Give up bacon and learn to love broccoli. In my search for new and interesting food, I discovered pristine all-white turnips that look like porcelain globes and taste sugary; mild, succulent golden beets that leave no stains on the tablecloth; and an arcane, delicious way to cook rutabagas with sauerkraut and garlic.

Scripture bears out the idea; other than the Ten Commandments, most of the law of Moses deals with physical health: avoid eating scavengers such as swine and hawks, don't eat bloody meat, don't boil a kid in its mother's milk. Keep people with infectious skin diseases outside your camp; stay away from dead bodies and have a latrine outside the camp, which you cover with dirt; refrain from sex during the menstrual period. All those laws prevented hepatitis, life-destroying parasites, undulant fever, bacterial skin and stomach disorders including ulcers, and probably cancers. The Hebrews took baths sprinkled with ashes—a mild lye solution—and mixed ash with fat (soap).

Balance between Care and Carefree

Does all this really matter at our age? What do we have to lose by smoking or eating poorly and becoming couch potatoes? Won't we simply enjoy ourselves, eat what we want, then die a little sooner—a sort of "I had it my way" ending?

Life and death don't work that way. What can happen if you don't tend your own body is diabetes and amputation of one or both feet. Or maybe a stroke that lands you in a nursing home for several years, unable to speak or move, maybe with a feeding tube and sometimes lying in your own pee. Or you can sit in a chair, staring at the TV and waiting for Meals on Wheels. Although some of these events can happen to non-smokers and people who stay fit, the scales are tilted against those who neglect their health.

Food plays an awfully important role. Studies at Baylor, Duke, and Stanford universities reveal that in order to slow the aging process, you should consume color. Crimson apples, tomatoes with scarlet cheeks, peppers of every hue, rosy or white-fleshed peaches, golden winter squash, blue-purple cabbage and radicchio, garnet yams and chartreuse broccoflower. And you have to have green things: asparagus, bok choy, spinach, kale, collards, chard, and every other substance that's full of chlorophyll and vitamin A. Some recent studies at important universities even suggest that blueberries and Concord grape juice might actually help brains stay alert.

And maybe avocados, beets, red grapes, and sweet potatoes contribute to mental strength.

So is that cheese Danish you eat for breakfast really worth the "unused life" you'll have to carry around as you plod into old age? Or would you rather walk erect into the good night? You can live longer and more fully, according to Deepak Chopra, M.D., the celebrated endocrinologist. Chopra ran Massachusetts General Hospital until he saw too many people with preventable ailments and wrote *Quantum Healing*. In a later volume, *Ageless Body, Timeless Mind*, Chopra insists we can live until age 120, and live fully. In that book, he suggests that the requirements for a long and healthy life are fresh food, pure water and air, sunlight, moderate exercise, good breathing (whatever that means), nonviolent behavior, reverence for life, loving, positive emotions, and free expression.

Well, I doubt that every single person who takes that list seriously will live past a hundred; but no item on it is either detrimental to health or opposed to God. And I suspect that "reverence for life" might change a lot of people so that God can begin operating in their heads.

Throughout his book, Chopra also emphasizes creativity, and I suspect that creativity may be a powerful

aspect in maintaining youthfulness. When you stay creative, you stay young, so get out those watercolors or
enroll in the dance class you've thought about. The
painter Pablo Picasso and the great cellist Pablo Casals
died at more than ninety years of age, and both worked
up until the last moments of their lives. They did what
we all hope to do: they lived until they died.

Whenever I want to use old age as an excuse for
being sedentary, I make myself remember Hildegard of
Bingen, who was seventy years old when she *walked* from
her German monastery to Paris so that she could show
her medical book to doctors at the Sorbonne. And
Hildegard, always outspoken, never lost her sharp tongue
in the face of heresy or hypocrisy. Like her sister saint,
Teresa of Ávila, Hildegard exhorted popes, kings, monks,
and mendicants, urging them to give money into the
bosom of the church and to reform religious orders. In
1979, John Paul II declared that she was a "light to her
people and her time, shining out more brightly today."

Well, if you want to be a light to your people, you
have to eat right, rest, stay creative, and—sigh—exercise.
Exercise isn't always easy, but you have to do as much as
you can, which may be more than you think. I remember
a time in my life when I was too miserable to eat or walk

or even talk. And then I read about then television host Dave Garroway, who was with his five-year-old son in a hotel room at the shore; he was trying to cope with his wife's untimely death. The little boy was bored and restless, and he said to Garroway, "Daddy? Come out and walk on the beach with me."

Garroway shook his head and the child pleaded. "I can't, son," he told the boy. "I'm just too tired."

The little boy sat on the edge of the bed a while, and then said, "Daddy? Will you just come walk with me till you fall down?"

God is asking me to turn back from indolence and walk until I fall down. And when I do, God will gently set me on my feet again. No matter what I'm trying to do, walk two blocks or run a marathon, failure is momentary and grace abounds within it.

So if you're joining me in the quest for a body worthy of resurrection, be at peace inside and out, rest and meditate on God, eat your vegetables, and walk until you fall down.

PART II

Looking Inward

❦

You desire truth in the inward being;
therefore teach me wisdom in my secret heart.

Psalm 51:6

CHAPTER SIX

The Night

If I make my bed in hell, behold, thou art there.
Psalm 139:8 KJV

"Con esto, mal dormir, todo trabajo, todo cruz!"
(And then, the scant sleep they get: nothing but
trials, nothing but crosses!)
St. Teresa of Ávila

SHABBAT NOTWITHSTANDING, SLEEP ISN'T always automatic. When I was a little girl, I was taught to recite when I woke up, "Today, everything is for you, God." Now it's time to say, as I stretch my legs down, down under the covers, almost touching the footboard with my toes, *Tonight, everything is for you; tonight, you may invade my soul and quicken my spirit, you may nearly suffocate me under a ton of Presence, you may engulf and instruct me. . . .*

Of course, the trick is to keep from adding, *but please don't keep me awake while you do it.*

Restless Bodies

Night is probably one of the hardest parts of aging. Between lying awake a lot and having too many dreams when we do drift off, our beds are no longer places just for rest or sex. The bed has become a battlefield where we fight for sleep. We often lie awake or sleep too lightly or dream too much, and most of those times, we have a hard time finding any spiritual benefit.

A popular myth says that older people need less sleep, and that the reason they're awake so much is that they've already had enough rest. Well, when you wake up after one hour, that doesn't mean you've had enough sleep. You're awake because your body is changing, and it sometimes gets its signals crossed. The wrong neurotransmitters sometimes surge forward, telling you to rise in the middle of the night, manic and creative, telling you to make phone calls or whip up a batch of crêpes suzette. You surely don't carry out those crazy commands, but you probably don't go back to sleep right away either. And on some nights maybe your legs start up, telling you that they must move, must keep moving, and they jerk you awake if you inadvertently slumber.

One of novelist Gabriel García Márquez's books tells about how one of the characters had to drink a shot of whiskey every morning because of the "burden of the night." Most of us older people don't wake up drinking anything stronger than half-decaf coffee, but the words may ring a bell somewhere inside your rib cage. Some evenings you probably even stay up too late because you dread the burden of the night.

And if you talk about sleep to ten other people over the age of sixty, at least eight of them will complain. They don't get enough rest so they're often sleepy in the afternoon. Some of us lie awake at the beginning of the night, our minds leaping from memory to memory or anxiety to anxiety, so that we can't fall asleep. Others of us go to sleep and wake several times, sometimes staying awake for two or three hours. Still others waken at, say, 3:00 A.M. and finally sleep after sunrise and have to stay in bed until ten—or they get up at 3:00 A.M. and stay tired all day.

Doctors say that the average total sleep time increases slightly after age sixty-five. But so do reports of difficulty falling asleep. People who are aging produce lesser amounts of certain chemicals that regulate the sleep cycle. Both melatonin (a substance that promotes sleep and is produced by the pineal gland) and growth hormone production decrease with age. Changes in body temperature occur: you have to cool down to sleep, and that cooling faculty slows down.

Because many aging people don't get outside as much as they should, the decrease in exposure to natural light can exacerbate sleep difficulties. Add to that the theory that daytime inactivity and lack of exercise—and maybe decreased mental stimulation—may lead to problems in falling asleep.

An aging bladder or an enlarged prostate contributes to a substantial degree of sleep disturbance, and the tendency to feel sleepier during the day than you did when you were younger results from these increased nocturnal awakenings. Our bodies are chronically uncomfortable; the dull edge of pain makes it impossible to sleep for a while. Aching joints, restless legs, tingling diabetic feet, and backs that have spent too many years walking upright don't merely hurt: intense pain can make us upset and half crazy. We wake in the middle of the night because we don't sleep as deeply in old age, and the slightest noise can penetrate our rest.

Haunted Minds

Besides physical changes, old age brings on renewed guilt. We tend to lie awake at night, reviewing our lives, guilty about the past and anxious about the future. If we have kids, we remember the times we were mean or impatient or unloving. We look back at mistakes in marriage or friendship. We agonize over the bad investment thirty years earlier that means today we're not as well off as we should be. The old Scottish prayer *From ghoulies and ghosties and long-leggity beasties and things that go bump in the night, Good Lord, deliver us!* speaks volumes about old age. Ghoulies dig up the graves of our guilt and the ghosties of our past; the phantoms of our younger years that we like to keep tucked away into the unconscious rise up again to haunt our sleepless nights; the long-leggity beasties that stalk us most as we're trying to fall asleep are negative memories trying to overwhelm all the good ones.

Then there's the terror that you'll die with your home a mess or your work unfinished. One evening I felt so terrible that I stayed up more than half the night, somehow finishing an important writing assignment, completely cleaning up my horrendous desk, and putting fresh sheets on my bed. If I should die before I wake, I reasoned, I wanted things to be in good shape. So I didn't fall in bed until after four, and then when I did, I was overstimulated and didn't sleep until dawn; but my desk was empty, and I'd finished a long article—just in case. The Psalmist's assurance that "It is in vain that you rise up early / and go late to rest, / eating the bread of anxious toil; / for he gives sleep to his beloved" (127:2) apparently doesn't apply to those of us who have gray hairs. The bread of anxious toil gets harder to earn, too: I work a lot more slowly than I did twenty or even ten years ago.

And probably the ultimate reason for sleeplessness stands at the foot of every older person's bed, shaking a bony finger. Where once we lay shivering in fear of what life might bring next, now we try to gird ourselves for death. Wondering how long you'll live—and how long you'll function—can keep you awake for a long time; you can stay up even longer, wondering if you'll die of cancer or stroke or kidney failure. Our generation is scared to death of protracted extraordinary life support, but we're also worried about the process of dying. "If I should die before I wake," which may not have meant too much to the average American child, takes on new meaning and makes fear our bedfellow.

What is all this sleep and dream business about? If you're forty or fifty, you may not know yet; if you're seventy, you probably understand. Sure, we read about the eighty-year-old man who has a saltwater farm in Maine, spends ten hours shearing and feeding the sheep while his wife spins the yarn and tans the skins for their Sherpa jackets; both of them sleep like babies until four-thirty every morning, when they get up to milk the cows. All that busyness makes me shiver; most of us over sixty are in poorer health than the Maine couple and have less self-discipline; and most of us have aches and pains or emotional concerns that can keep us from deep sleep.

Redeemed Time

But the problem of sleep in old age is ultimately not so much how to overcome wakefulness, but how to redeem the time. As I said in the last chapter, our assignment is to give meaning to the time we're on earth, and that includes the nights. The night was made for prayer, whether it be the prayer of *Don't let me die* or *Show me your Glory, God.*

Although you could get a prescription for something that will make you drowsy and set your TV sleep timer and drift off with Larry King dribbling into your dreams, that combination of soporifics can be addictive. Even without the pills; a writer friend of mine calls TV the most dangerous addiction in the country, and he may be right. You can probably quit smoking or munching potato chips, but can you toss the TV down the steps?

Sometimes you may lie awake because God has something to say and can't get your attention during the daylight hours. Several years ago, Fleming Revell published a book by Connie Soth, titled *Insomnia: God's Night School.* She didn't delve too deeply into the whys of wakefulness—her book was meant for insomniacs of all ages—but she talked at length about what can happen in the dark and how the night can belong to the journey toward holiness. She was right: the night can hold a great deal of schooling. Psalm 16 says that in the night "my heart instructs me." The Psalmist was listening to his own heart because he knew that the "heart"—not necessarily the pump in his chest, but the seat of knowledge and wisdom in the human organism—contained his handbook for life.

If all the cells in your body, every scrap of hair or slough of skin, contain your entire DNA code, then maybe your "heart" is everywhere, too, in your lips and fingertips and feet, in your brain and in your dreams. The Psalmist's "night instruction" probably isn't just prayer and thinking and meditation and longing; I think he was also talking about dreams, those mysterious forays into another space and time. Dreams disturb sleep not by keeping us awake, but by locking us into terror or wonder or, occasionally, heaven. I sometimes wake from a dream exhausted by remembrance.

Telling Dreams

Dreams matter to people all over the world. Perhaps the reason that nonindustrial cultures consider old people wise is that they dream so much. Many believers in Islam show great reverence to a man asleep, because his dreams are holy, and people who dream frequently are sacred and chosen intermediaries between the deity and man.

My own aging dreamer is certainly active: I think I must be dreaming all night, every night, and taking in immense quantities of teaching from myself and God. My dreams are more vivid and more direct every year, and I think God is the impresario of my nightlife. Emerson's remark that "Mysticism consists in the mistake of an accidental and individual symbol for an universal one" must have been uttered when he was young, because age is mystical and dreams are an important way in which God talks to us. Lately, I've dreamed a lot about houses: about the one I live in, or some I have lived in, or some with strange big rooms and hidden cubbies. Sometimes I'm moving to a new place, finding secret rooms in the one I have, hunting through the house for something I've lost (probably just a reflection of my days: I'm always losing my glasses or car keys, and before I go to an appointment I sometimes rush wildly about the house, praying to St. Anthony to show me where to look). Dreams about houses usually have something to do with one's life or lifestyle. Last night I dreamed about a house I was trying to move into, and a tyrannical landlord who kept pushing me and my belongings out, and I wonder what I'm telling myself. Am I just telling myself to be firm about keeping extraneous issues out of my life, or is the landlord what the Hero's Journey would call a "threshold guardian," someone who keeps you from taking the next step? And is the next step writing another book—or death?

Sometimes we all have what some psychologists call "lucid dreams," when we know we are dreaming. Sometimes I tell myself that I'll refuse to wake up because of how delightful the dream is, and at other times I try desperately to open my eyes or move my arms so I can escape the terrible imagery.

The *Catholic Encyclopedia* says, "In the light of the belief and practices of the ancient peoples, we are better able to judge the belief and practices recorded in the Bible. That God may enter into communication with man through dreams is asserted in Numbers 12:6 and still more explicitly in Job 33:14–18:

> *For God speaks in one way,*
>> *and in two, though people do not*
>> *perceive it.*
> *In a dream, in a vision of the night,*
>> *when deep sleep falls on mortals,*
>> *while they slumber on their beds,*
> *then he opens their ears,*
>> *and terrifies them with warnings,*

that he may turn them aside from their
deeds, and keep them from pride,
to spare their souls from the Pit,
their lives from traversing the River.

God sent a message through dreams to Pharaoh and Abimelech and St. Joseph and St. Peter. Apparently they had no doubt that their dreams or "night visions" were any different from ordinary dreams in which the dreamer rehashes the day's events or rehearses personal fears and desires. And in Genesis 40:8, Joseph says, "Do not interpretations belong to God?"

Heavenly Glimpses

Dreams are life or death, and in older age, we sometimes want to stay with them, make them our true existence. In Sonnet 2 of Sonnets to Orpheus, the poet Rainer Maria Rilke wrote

She dreamed the world. Singing God, how
made you that primordial repose so sound

she never felt a need to waken? Upon
arising she fell straight to dream. Where is
her death? O, will you yet discover her
theme before your song is eclipsed forever?

Though you make your bed in hell, you glimpse heaven in your dreams. You will still hear God and the angels singing into the hot darkness, and the words to the angels' song are the same words God spoke to bring the universe into being and to give human life to the Son.

If you approach every night with dread, things won't get better; in fact, you'll exacerbate the situation. The only answer is to cope with it differently every twenty-four hours, to come to bed with delighted anticipation of God's presence. It's all a matter of spontaneity. Each time you walk toward the bed, try to think *New: a new night, a new dream.* Maybe a new set of problems, but very likely also a new time of talking to God, a new, revealing dream that might give you a glimpse of heaven. Just remember what the jazz singer Billie Holliday said:

I can't stand to sing the same song the same
way two nights in succession, let alone two

years or ten years. If you can, then it ain't
music, it's close-order drill or exercise or
yodeling or something, not music.

Night and night prayer surely deserve more than a close-order drill. You've got to sing a mental song into the night, because if you can stand to think the same thoughts every night as you pull up the covers, that ain't music, and it sure ain't sung by angels.

CHAPTER SEVEN

Pleasure

So Sarah laughed to herself, saying,
"After I have grown old, and my husband is old,
shall I have pleasure?"

Genesis 18:12

The greater part of our happiness or our misery
depends on our dispositions
and not on our circumstances.

Martha Washington, first First Lady of the United States

JUST A FEW MOMENTS AGO I POURED TEA from my favorite pot, and I felt a surge of delectation. Whenever I use that teapot, I get to relive my last birthday, when my son and his wife took me and a beautiful wine-and-cheese supper to a place where you buy greenware, glaze it, and have it fired. We spent the evening eating, drinking, and painting. I used blue for the background of the small teapot and its matching rounded

cup, then painted small colorful flowers on it. Its color
and proportions delight my eye. So does the memory of
that evening of china painting, red wine, Brie, and the
company of family.

The Pleasure of Everyday Things

Pleasure isn't difficult if you don't set impossible goals
and you learn to take your delight in small things—and
in new ones. Ten years ago I didn't know the names of
many birds besides our noisy black ravens and brilliant
blue jays and fat robins; but now, with the help of a pair
of thirty-dollar binoculars and an Audubon book, I can
identify pine siskins, bushtits, varied thrushes, cedar
waxwings, and warblers that cavort in the trees and
brambles behind my house. The sight of a migrating
trumpeter swan or snow goose, winging overhead, gives
me the same degree of relish as chocolate tiramisu. I get
a thrill every May, watching bright-colored little
goldfinches arrive here. I can sit in my den and watch as
they surge from alder to maple tree at the edges of our

Douglas fir woods. They usually stay a week or two, and I watch them turn into yellow leaves on the trees and take sudden high, swarming flights.

I have a thirteen-year-old camera and a more recent macro lens that can bring the very stamens of a flower into focus; as a result, I have slides of nearly every blooming wild plant in Oregon. I don't have to travel to exotic places to have exotic experiences. Taking snapshots of street carnivals and convoluted neon signs and night-blooming cactus is so outré for me that I might as well be in Damascus or Paris. When I was younger, impatience and energy might have kept me from such simple pleasures as looking at goldfinches or the blue petals of wild iris; the very slowness of aging has made me more able to look and receive. Slowness has helped but so has remembering the words of Yoda from *Star Wars:* "There is no *try.* There is only do."

Just as I take delight in my teapot and the brisk Yorkshire tea imported from England, I enjoy a great assortment of music, everything from Paul Hindemith to Charlotte Church's "I Vow to Thee, My Country" to Laura Nyro's "Stoney End." And I felt frissons of pleasure when, during the millennium celebration, I saw on TV people of Tonga turn their faces to the dawn and sing the Hallelujah Chorus. I sang it over and over again, all that day.

I revel in the rise of woods behind my house, and recently I took some interested historians on a hike into the hills where, in those very woods, a tiny cemetery with six partly broken headstones hides under the trees. Once people had cleared land and raised a homestead there; now, both they and the homestead are gone; but their record remains. I took pictures of those tombstones, and when I got home, aching and thirsty, covered with grass particles and fir needles, my skin scarred by wicked blackberry brambles, I discovered a great celebration in my heart.

The difference between pleasure and joy is a big one. You can be pleasure deprived and still experience joy, because joy is a decision. Or you can buy into every small pleasure you can, and still lack joy. One may or may not lead to the other.

What you must decide is whether you're going to look for reasons to celebrate. What I call a "celebration life" has to embrace not only the spiritual but all the elements of daily life, from your steaming oatmeal in the morning to your favorite pillow at bedtime. No matter how glorious the perception, no matter how gratifying the event, nothing is ever truly fulfilling until you draw closer to God and enter the mystical temple God placed within you.

Food, cooking, and tasting are occupations of some older people, partly because now that we're retired or semi-retired, with fewer demands on our time, we can play in our kitchens. Moncy is only as good as what you do with it, and if you attend a French cooking or wine-tasting class, you can bring home knowledge and fun. I throw fresh fennel and baby bok choy and handfuls of whole, peeled garlic into my stir-fry, having branched out a lot from the old days, when carrots, celery, a sprinkle of ginger, and some button mushrooms were what made Asian food. I go to a local tearoom that serves a high tea with scones, petits fours, and tiny sandwiches. I could eat thirty-four of their ginger-chicken creations on miniature buns.

Now that our kids are grown up, we no longer eat artery-clogging fast food; instead of cheeseburgers, we can go to the farmer's market and pick up fresh cilantro, baby spinach, and Yukon gold potatoes. By now, you've probably experimented with Japanese green tea and maybe even read *Laurel's Kitchen,* and while you delight your aging palate, you can also make your body happy to have all those antioxidants.

The Pleasure of Remembrance

As you get older you discover great pleasure in remembering; in fact, you can create a kind of virtual memory book. On one of my mental "pages" is the day after last Thanksgiving, when I was visiting my daughter in North Carolina. We got up at six that Friday, dressed in a hurry, and were in a store, Christmas shopping, at seven! At ten we had brunch and shopped some more. I spent a lot of money, but the real pleasure of my memory comes from our laughter and closeness, from the decorations in the stores, from a few wild bargains and our brunch. I can still taste that hot croissant, the homemade raspberry jam, and the fresh coffee, all consumed in a restaurant full of plants and Christmas music.

And I remember a picnic we had thirty years ago on a high bank above the North Umpqua River near Roseburg, Oregon. We heard music and looked down through the trees to watch a baptism. The little congregation sang "Shall We Gather at the River" while one after another, people in white garments were thrust under the rushing water and raised to new life. My best memory of that day is the ecstatic face of one young woman who, when she came out of the water, smiled so as to equal starlight, stretched her arms toward her husband on the bank, and cried, "Oh, Jimmy . . ."

I'll always hold onto big and small memories: the first time I held each of my babies in my arms; a plate of fresh trout we ate beside a campfire; standing in the Sistine Chapel; carrying a cross up the Via Dolorosa in Jerusalem. When I was a teenager, I ushered for the Good Friday long performance of Wagner's opera *Parsifal;* if you ushered, you were allowed to *stand* through the eight-hour performance.

Get out your journal and start writing down which memories taste best on your memory's tongue: the day your first child married, or the time you skied downhill on a bright winter day when the sun turned the snow into a hill of diamonds. Perhaps you'll want to jot down some restaurant suppers or family breakfasts or the Sundays in church when you distributed communion. And how about the best books you ever read?

I was an only child with chronic breathing problems, so I learned at a young age that it's fun to read, even when friends are playing outside. Reading has to be the easiest way to transport yourself into other times and places, to identify with very different people, and sometimes to experience the joy of learning. Last summer I read Barbara Kingsolver's novel, *Prodigal Summer*, and I am, months later, still wrapped in that beautiful prose.

One day I made a list of the childhood books I had read and reread. Many of them were old when I was young: my aging godmother gave me all her books she'd enjoyed as a child in the 1890s. For my eighth birthday she presented me with a new edition of her own childhood favorite, *The Book of Live Dolls*, a trilogy about a village in the Midwest where the Fairy Queen brings all the dolls to life. I read it and read it and read it. By the time I was eleven or twelve I shifted to *A Tale of Two Cities*, *Green Mansions*, *My Name Is Aram*, and *How Green Was My Valley*. But they didn't enchant me in the same way, and the memory of what I read as a child has lingered all my life. I don't know just what became of my old books, so after I made my list, I started looking on eBay and other online resources. Now I have copies of every one of my favorite books, including *The Book of Live Dolls*, which electrifies me the same way it did when I was eight. What were your favorites? And why not find and reread them, to stimulate the child that still lives in you?

But you can't limit pleasure to memory. You have to constantly refresh it; you've got to be present to what feels or tastes or sounds good. You have to create new experiences and thus new memories. The pleasure of human contact changes as you age. I think most of us would now prefer tea with one or two dear friends to the big, noisy party that was fun for us at thirty-five. Maybe that's because relationships in old age are shot through with death; you don't have another fifty years to go to parties and visit pals. You might not see your great-grandchild graduate from college, and none of us will see the next century, either January 1, 2100 or 2101, depending on which camp you belong to. Death is always present in relationships, but sometimes you don't realize that until you turn seventy. The older you get, the more effort you make in some relationships (and the less effort in those that have no apparent promise).

Sometimes friendships you might have with younger people are a pleasure to them. Oliver Wendell Holmes, in a graduation speech at Harvard, said, "A man over ninety is a great comfort to all his elderly neighbors: he is a picket-guard at the extreme outpost; and the young folks of sixty and seventy feel that the enemy must get by him before he can come near their camp."

So a cup of coffee and a scone at the bakery with a friend you haven't seen for a while can become a banquet within your spirit, because the very fact of death makes life more delicious. Playing cribbage with your old pal from next door is the kind of fun you had when you were both kids and you wet-knotted your other friend's underwear when he hung it on a limb and dived into the swimming hole. And a stroll through the woods with your spouse might now equal the pleasure of the honeymoon you took years ago.

The Pleasure of Sex

Which brings us to sex. Because no matter how old you are or what your circumstances, sex produces the greatest pleasure known to humans, and much of what we do and say and think, consciously or otherwise, rises out of sexuality. Is sexuality during aging a secret or just something nobody wants to look at? How often do we turn on the TV to see a couple of aging bodies covered with sweat and wallowing around in the covers? In a tone of surprise, Michigan's *Holland Sentinel* printed this headline over a study of older people and sex: "The truth: Old folks still have sex." I doubt that the astonished headline was written by anyone over the age of fifty-five.

Women often become more interested in sex as they get older. After menopause they don't have to check their calendars or their secretions to avoid pregnancy, and they often get a surge of hormonal activity in midlife. Since in their minds nobody ever, ever feels their age after about thirty-five, nothing inside us says, "All right, now you're sixty. Maybe you had good sex with your spouse yesterday, but today that's all over." If sex is ever all over it's because of death or illness, not the cessation of desire.

Sex is, however, more complicated in older age. Most of us prefer the dark, where the ravages of age on our bodies is not so conspicuous. I heard a TV commentator say that once her motto was "Look, but don't touch"; now she thinks, "Touch, but don't look." And that attitude isn't just so your spouse isn't discouraged by sagging flesh, but so you can feel beautiful. In the dark, I can pretend I'm still a slender girl with long legs and blond hair, a girl who knew she was pretty. And in the dark, you can pretend your partner is still young and desirable. When you both feel beautiful, you arouse and participate more easily.

But appearance is only a small complication. A bigger one is the effect of aging—and the illnesses of aging—on our organs. Men with diabetes and prostate problems and other circulatory disorders are often impotent; and many cannot—because of heart trouble or medicines or other conditions—take "miracle" drugs like Viagra. And many men who can't either achieve or maintain that necessary stimulated state often forget about affection and touching or possibly satisfying their wives a different way.

Patricia Bloom, M.D., of St. Luke's–Roosevelt Hospital Center in New York City suggests that sexual activity is one of those stimulating kinds of activity that may promote brain function in elderly people. She cites some data suggesting that men who have many orgasms may live a longer life, although she says she suspects that what's really true is that men who are healthy enough to be very sexually active don't have underlying severe diseases, and therefore do live a longer life. "I don't think that the sex causes you to live longer," she says, "but I think it's correlated with living longer."

Women can have their own organic discomforts after menopause and are sometimes reluctant to engage in sexual activity because it's painful. Eventually, a couple may give up sex because the difficulty outweighs the pleasure so that, Bob Dole's encouragement notwithstanding, a number of married couples in this country are leading unhappily celibate lives. I know devout Catholic women who pleasure themselves because their husbands can no longer function. They feel guilty, go to confession, and repeat the cycle. One woman who is widowed says she hasn't had to struggle to remain celibate as far as other men are concerned; but, she adds, red faced, that she sometimes relieves herself.

Whether you are single and celibate, or married and unhappily celibate, remember that God is good and will inject into your life other kinds of love, other brands of relationship, and pleasures in art and reading and music and memory.

Sure, sex is the basic means of procreation, but it is also a means of delight between husband and wife; sex nourishes and seals marriage. When Sarah heard the angels say that she would become pregnant, she didn't say, "At my age, I can conceive?" She laughed and said, "After I have grown old, and my husband is old, shall I have pleasure?" When God asked Sarah why she laughed, and she denied it, I think she was embarrassed—the very thought of intercourse was so pleasurable she laughed aloud.

Why was she—in fact, why are we—so scared and shamefaced when we admit that we long for physical and emotional enjoyment? C. S. Lewis says the very fact of our embarrassment shows that sex is at the very center of our fallenness. We murmur about sex, we snigger about sex, but how many times have you heard a sermon glorifying sex as the pleasure bond between husbands and wives? Even though sex appears hundreds of times every day on television and in movies, even though the term "oral sex" was tossed about as easily as "tonight's news" by the press during the Clinton years, most of us have some sense of shame about sex and its pleasure.

But sex symbolizes the uniting of heaven and earth. No wonder God implanted in us such a capacity for pleasure in sex, then. The problem is that we prefer to keep God outside the bedroom because of our shame connected to it. God and sex are two inseparable mysteries, and they can combine as one immediate pleasure. Pope John Paul II's theology of the body is a clarion call for Christians today to become not more spiritual but more incarnational. We can't understand the Christian mystery unless we understand the mystery of our bodies, the mystery of sexuality, the mystery of marriage.

And from the mystery of our bodies, we have to turn toward those whose bodies are even more mysterious, bodies that won't move or function or take us from one place to another. People with strokes or ALS or stage-four cancer or rheumatoid arthritis. They perhaps discovered sooner than the rest of us that one pleasure is easier to achieve and lasts longer than any other: prayer.

The Pleasure of Prayer

You can live without sex if you have to. You can live without the pleasures of running or gourmet cooking or art museums. But the one deep, satisfying pleasure necessary for any kind of life is prayer: adoring, praising, thanking, pleading. In another chapter, I'll talk about prayer at greater length, but for now I explore its relation to pleasure. If you allow yourself the ecstasy of intimacy with God, your life will be full of pleasure, along with the sense of God's joy in what you do.

If you let it, prayer can bring intense, even physical pleasure. Give yourself up to the presence of God, and God will transport you into ecstasy. This only happens when you're really praying and doing nothing else. The quick blessing you mutter as you turn the key in your ignition, or the kinds of anxious petitions that come when you're trying to clamber out of a deep love seat don't usually bring any rapture. Transports of delight accompany wordless prayers when, as St. Teresa of Ávila described her experience, you look at God and God looks at you. Pleasure comes in prayer when you have a nanosecond-long glimpse of seeing God face to face. This is the joy St. Thomas Aquinas hoped for when he wrote, "Jesus, whom now veiled, I by faith decry, What my soul doth thirst for, do not, Lord, deny, That thy face unveiled, I at last may see, With the blissful vision blest, my God, of thee" (*Adoro Devote*, "Humbly I adore thee"; Thomas Aquinas, 1225?–1274).

Prayer offers its own rewards, so long as it is prayer that seeks only God and not some other end. God loves to dollop happiness and ecstasy on anyone who will go before the throne for no other reason than to worship.

And pleasure comes not only from prayer, but from obedience: not the drudgery of keeping a rule, but of being what God made you to be. Perhaps the greatest line ever uttered in a movie was in *Chariots of Fire*, when Ian tells his sister, "The Lord also made me fast; and when I run, I feel his pleasure." And Mechtilde of Magdeburg, that thirteenth-century Beguine who called Christ her playmate, said, "Love penetrates the senses and storms the soul with all its power. . . . Love melts through the soul and into the senses. And so the body, too, gains its part and conforms in all ways to love."

CHAPTER EIGHT

Can Older Be Holier?

I appeal to you therefore, brothers and sisters, by the
mercies of God, to present your bodies as a living
sacrifice, holy and acceptable to God, which is your
spiritual worship. Do not be conformed to this
world, but be transformed by the renewing of your
minds, so that you may discern what is the will of
God—what is good and acceptable and perfect.

Romans 12:1– 2

HOLINESS ON EARTH IS JUST A REHEARSAL, after all. Just as lion cubs leap and pounce in their baby games not just to play but to learn how to someday hunt their food, so human beings play at heaven. We fall in love to learn to live in the presence of Love; we take Communion to practice for the wedding supper of the Lamb; we exercise ourselves in prayer to get ready to speak to God face to face. Life is practice for eternity, and what we learn to live in life is what we'll take into the next world.

God is sending pictures of holiness into our lives, every day.

Looking for God

When I moved into this house eight years ago, I planted a tiny snowball bush outside my office window. It's now taller than the house, and its colors pervade the room where I work eight or nine hours a day. In the spring, lush blossoms make even my dark desk reflect the white snowballs. In summer, sunshine on the abundant leaves converts my smallish workroom into a conservatory or greenhouse. And in fall, the brilliant foliage splashes my windows with red, orange, and yellow and warms my heart for the coming winter.

I think I would write differently without that bush. Its delicate May colors make me more poetic in my expression. The deep green of summer enriches my definition of creation. And the glorious tints of autumn, coloring my working world, lift my heart and mind toward God with a greater sense of adoration and joy.

In the same way, the hues of God's presence adorn aging, making light dance on the walls of our spirits and calling us to holiness. On days when we have more trouble getting in touch with God, a holy life is possible, if only through our relationships. Macrina Wiederkehr, in her book *A Tree Full of Angels,* speaks of days when all you do is look for God, search high and low for God, and wonder where God is. Wiederkehr always finds God eventually, sometimes within herself but often in nature or other people.

Do you ever spend a day searching high and low for God? Finding God, being in the presence of God, means being holy enough for the experience. But before you decide you're not good enough to go searching, ask yourself what holiness is. How do you live the rest of your life in sanctity? Must a person pray every minute, reading from a pocket Bible or prayer book even during a meeting of the city council? Should one become ascetic, cleaning out the house and garage, shedding all but two outfits of clothes, a bed, and a table? (And can you easily convince a pack-rat spouse to do this?) Must we attend church not only on Sunday but at every midweek service? Should we confine ourselves to nothing but "religious" experience?

Well, no. Those things point not toward holiness but piety—and possibly a shallow piety at that. Holiness is beyond religion and may not have a lot of outer evidences except compassion for others. To be holy means to take the Sacred with you wherever you go, to see the Sacred everywhere you stand, and to search out God within every human being you encounter, whether it be the homeless woman who picks through the dumpster or the guy next door mowing his lawn.

It is no accident that the words *holy* and *whole* sound alike, because they have the same root. To seek a life of holiness means to see wholeness—not only in oneself but in other people and even in creation. Holiness loves everything as God loves it and sees life as God intended it to be. What is sacred, what is godly, is whole and not fragmented or tattered.

Jesus is always whole. His body was pierced. His image hanging over an ancient church altar may get beaten up by time: its paint may chip, the wood may warp, the image may splinter from too many falls to the church's stone floor. But Jesus Christ himself is not battered or chipped, and his soul was never pierced. He is entire, whole, complete, and unchanging. And it is in this true image that we and all other human beings were made.

Erik Erikson, the psychologist-philosopher who has delineated the stages of life—and who, with his wife, Joan, traveled and wrote to explain the importance of coming to terms with each stage of the life cycle—was fond of saying, "No less than a whole life." Translate *whole* into *holy* and you have the description of the life God asks us to lead. Isn't that what we're in this for in the first place? God is our subject and verb. God is beyond our lives and yet passionately entwined in them. The life I live, God lives also. Therefore, unless I want to drag God into the gutter, I have to choose what is Christlike, that which is like the life in our heavenly home.

The words of the Our Father that speak of God's kingdom coming to earth as it has in heaven mean that we can have the kingdom. The kingdom and the grace and the wholeness of heaven. Our joy in God is God's joy in us; or, as Meister Eckehart said somewhere, "The eye by which I see God is the eye by which God sees me." And since everyone in heaven is whole, let the kingdom come.

❧

Journeying Inward

"Home" rarely means a place you've never seen; it's a place where you've been and where you return. But we're somewhat like Palestinians who, though born in a refugee camp, speak of "home," meaning the town or village their grand-parents came from but which they, themselves, have never visited. I don't know whether we were with God before we were born, but I know where home is.

Heaven is home and holiness is our natural state, so what about original sin? Well, it didn't start in heaven! We became subject to sin by being born into a broken and confused world. But faith in Jesus removes that Adamic curse, and we're equipped for goodness. And it doesn't matter whether we were baptized yesterday or seventy years ago, God is still waiting to help us become saints. Saints have always been everywhere. An old children's hymn proclaims of the saints, "One was a doctor, and one was a queen, and one was a shepherdess on the green" and at the end of the verse adds, "And I want to be one, too."

A saint? Perfectible? Holy? Is this possible? Isn't humankind destined to be imperfect on earth?

John Wesley, the founder of Methodism, believed that human perfection was possible in an individual's life-time. This perfection, called holiness, was not a human achievement, however, but a gift from God. Wesley believed that if God could forgive sin, God could also transform the individual into a saint to lead a perfect and unflawed life. And if you won't believe a Methodist, then listen to the popular Catholic TV host Sister Angelica, who says, "We are all meant to be great saints." As we journey toward God, in this world and the next, we're meant to be holy.

When did holiness come to earth? At the moment God thought of creating the universe. But holiness, since it was then our natural state, was not mentioned in the Garden of Eden or anywhere in Genesis. The first historical reference to holiness occurs when God called Moses to preach to the Israelites and journey toward the Promised Land. Moses, first awed by the burning bush, heard the voice of God say, "Come no closer! Remove the sandals from your feet, for the place on which you are standing is holy ground." Moses had never known holiness before that moment, but he became a man who was consumed by it—so consumed that he talked to God face to face and his own countenance shone, so that he had to go about veiled. God put the longing for holiness within us; Moses introduced it to the other children of Israel; Jesus Christ lived it. And now we can put on Christ's holiness.

The first encouraging thing is that we find it easier to become saintly at seventy than at twenty. In older age we don't have so many physical temptations; for instance, we're not so quickly excited about sex. And we've gotten used to feeling what we feel, so that fewer of us have to start drowning ourselves in drugs or alcohol. Most of us don't have to look for an adrenaline rush by bungee jumping or skateboarding in pipes or running sixty yards with a football under our arm—all perfectly worthy experiences, but by their very nature, temptations toward pride or toward thinking we're the masters of our own lives and destinies. Many of us are too old to run for office or to try to become powerful in some other public way. Now, instead of climbing Mount Everest or the Matterhorn or some other famous peak, we can get our satisfaction from the journey inward. The trip to holiness.

Recognizing the Holy

The first step in that journey has to be the acknowledgment of the powerful—the recognition that God is present not just in our prayers or in the Host on our tongues but in every moment in human life. God pervades the atoms of the earth and everything and everyone in it. Even those who commit grievous sins and evil deeds have the breath of God in them and were made in the image of the Almighty. Knowing this should give a person who's lived here sixty or eighty years (and had a chance to observe the godliness of creation) an enhanced sense of the sacred. We are more able than the youthful souls around us to notice that not only the flowers in spring or the brightness of fall leaves are reminders of God, but we remember what physicists have told us: that every baby born, every puppy running between our feet, even every cat sitting on the backyard fence is made out of the stardust that burst forth at God's command. Creation is constant: God rested, but is back on the job.

Holiness can attain presence in our lives so long as our aging spirituality is a new phase of adventure with God, and not just a comfortable pew or prayer position to slip into. So long as we pine for the King James or Douay Bible, so long as we wish to sing only old hymns and listen to familiar words, preferably in an ancient language, we'll achieve consolation—but not holiness. Several years ago a Harris Poll found that while 71 percent of people of retirement age found religion "comforting" (compared with only 49 percent of younger people); the next most comforting element in their lives was, they said, "television." Considering the vapid content of most mass-media programs, "comforting religion" probably doesn't proclaim salvation or even hope. Holiness isn't the same as being comforted or comfortable. In fact, holy people often find Jesus Christ abrasive because he's always summoning them to higher ground, to harder climbing, and to deeper understanding.

Speaking of holiness versus comfort reminds me of a series PBS ran awhile back called *Stephen Hawking's Universe.* As I listened to the computer-generated voice of this remarkable man and viewed the accompanying photographs of galaxies and pulsars and other creatures of the heavens, I felt as if I were standing at the edge of divinity and mystery. I wasn't comforted—if anything, I was troubled, challenged, and overwhelmed—and I was filled with delight and a sense of quest. If a person can be so excited simply by looking at a galaxy that's six billion light years away, imagine how that same individual will react to the actual throne of God, which has been there since forever.

Unloading the Unimportant

Perhaps our next step in trying to live a holy life is to unload what we really don't need. The problem with achieving holiness in old age isn't just that we're all miserable sinners: it's also the baggage we lug around. Joseph Campbell once said that we must be willing to get rid of the life we've planned in order to have the life that is waiting for us. What an invitation! No matter how old I am and how practiced at life, God still has a better way for me, a holier way to live, a richer, fuller existence both here on earth and beyond. But I must drop my load. I can't live a new life while grasping the old one with both hands.

We all have psychological patterns and routinized emotional responses. We may be in the habit of praying in the context of need, rather than praying simply for communication's sake. And if we would be holy, if we would ready ourselves for heaven in such a way that we come to life's final gate in a state of grace, we have to dump all our ancient resentments—many a woman seventy years old is still angry at something her mother did when she was thirteen—and all our compulsive attachments. Life has to give way to the "purposeful emptiness" of Emma Benignus, described in another chapter.

For most people, unloading means also getting rid of some belongings, and what's more important, relinquishing things that are already lost. If you still mourn the cut-glass pitcher that you inherited from your grandmother and then broke, or the books you loaned that never came home, or the house you could have bought for a song and didn't (maybe because your spouse objected), it's time to divest yourself of those things. They're not yours, they've passed into history, and that pain you nurture is keeping you from the holy life that's waiting for you.

The other baggage we have to shed is judgment. We've got to divest ourselves of many beliefs about life, about laws, and about what other people do. Instead of judging people to be lazy and worthless, we have to bow to the Christ within them and treat them with compassion. We may have to decide that money isn't so important after all and that the political candidates who run on a money-inspired ticket might be wrong in God's eyes. We may have to take the Sermon on the Mount as our standard instead of accepting Wall Street's.

Engaging in Community

The third step of living as holy people is to engage in the faith community, because holiness isn't meant to be experienced alone, except perhaps for the few God has called to eremitic life. Communion and worship offer us rich opportunity in which to practice holiness, and the fellowship of the church community is an invitation to see God in that dialogue with other people. The church is the fellowship Paul describes in Colossians as a place where you can "let the peace of Christ rule in your hearts, to which indeed you were called in the one body . . . [letting] the word of Christ dwell in you richly; teach and admonish one another in all wisdom; and with gratitude in your hearts sing psalms, hymns, and spiritual songs to God" (3:15–16).

And holiness can't end at noon on Sunday, though it often appears to. We see families quarreling bitterly on their way home from church about where to go for lunch or how the driver is maneuvering through traffic or how someone behaved during the service, even after hearing the word of Christ and after singing those spiritual songs and psalms. America, so gifted in technology, has no idea how to live a sacred life. We're more excited by winning something, by being right, or by making a lot of money. But the coin of God's kingdom is not of this world: an awful lot of what America considers worthwhile is something that doesn't interest God. Yet we try to succeed here, rather than preparing for eternal life. The Gospel of Matthew tells us that the devil took Christ to a very high mountain and showed him all the kingdoms of the world and their splendor. "All these I will give you," he said to the Son of God, "if you will fall down and worship me." Wow! What a temptation. But Jesus answered immediately: "Away with you, Satan! for it is written, 'Worship the Lord your God, and serve him only'" (Matthew 4:8–10). Now what percentage of America do you think worships God and God only? How many of us can stay holy for even a whole day? Perhaps it's up to us, the elderly, who may have the experience to know that even the most exciting technologies come and go, and that there's another world ahead, to invite them into a greater community: that is, the gathering of saints.

In this world, our spirituality is put on trial. Paul, in his letter to Titus, says, "Tell the older men to be temperate, serious, prudent, and sound in faith, in love, and in endurance. Likewise, tell the older women to be reverent in behavior." This isn't so we'll look good to God—God knows what's inside us, after all—but so we'll be examples to the church. The "temperate, serious, prudent" man—who is so sound in faith that he holds his grandson on his lap during church and holds his wife's hand as they pray—is not only attractive; he invites imitation. And although we may not feel very holy in our hearts, acting holy can start us on the road to the real thing.

Putting on Christ

Holiness is not a season, but a state to strive for, a habit to learn. A holy life is no longer really your own; Christ's is the life to put on as a garment. "Putting on Christ," as Paul describes in the thirteenth chapter of Romans, doesn't mean trying to copy Jesus; it means trying to be Jesus. And that's the essence of a sacred life.

To put on Christ means thinking as Jesus thinks, as well as talking as he talks. You have to think compassion, truth, gentleness, and love. You have to become an instrument of healing for every person and situation. And ultimately you have to sacrifice yourself for those who don't deserve it. You may have been doing these things all your life, so now you intensify your efforts. Above all you have to have the inner Christ: the one who is in constant conversation with his Father, the one who knows God the way you know familiar things such as paper and grass. To put on Christ means to live in intimacy with God while existing in that same intimacy with our fellow men and women.

But to put on Christ is not to become nobody. Jesus said that he who loses his life will find it, and more recently the writer Robert Benson told a group, "When I look for God I find myself; when I look for myself, I find God."

CHAPTER NINE

Creativity and Your Spirit

Out of Zion, the perfection of beauty,
God shines forth.

Psalm 50:2

Hope is easier when it comes with a song.

Linda Clare

S HE LOOKED AS IF SHE HAD COME STRAIGHT
from James Agee's 1941 book, *Let Us Now Praise
Famous Men,* in which Walker Evans's poignant photographs show tragic, emaciated women of Appalachia.
But this person lives not far from me, in farmland not far
from a modern southern city, and she was having a quilt
sale in her yard.

She looked at me with disbelief when I said that I
didn't sew.

"You don't do no fancy work or rugs or *nothing?*" she asked, scandalized. Her front teeth were gone. She took me inside, showed me her cedar chest full of embroidered pillowcases with their tatted or crocheted edges, held up a quilt she was finishing, and then pointed to the frame where she was hooking a rug. I told her I used to do needlepoint but that too many years of typing and playing the piano had left me with carpal tunnel problems. But I could tell she was dubious about my basic character.

As I left, I heard her hiss to her husband, "That woman don't know how to keep busy."

I remembered my husband's grandmother telling me about her daily schedule on the farm: she washed on Monday, of course, and ironed on Tuesday, mended on Wednesday, baked on Thursday, and cleaned house from top to bottom. "I'd make the evening meal on those days," she said. "After I did the dishes, I'd sit on the porch and embroider until the light was too dim, and then I'd go in the house and work on braiding rugs."

Her needlework, like the quilt lady's, was art; but she didn't think of herself as creative. She just wanted to be industrious and productive. I longed to take her to a museum, to see quilts no better than hers; I even wanted to tell her that she was doing prayer, but she preferred to think of herself as keeping busy. And I think there's a trend, maybe even a plot, to keep old folks busy with meaningless little tasks that masquerade as craft.

If you really want to paint by number or make slippers, fine. But don't do busy work, or busy art. One of the worst Christian myths—or maybe even heresies—is that God wants you to occupy every moment of your time with some kind of work, even in (or especially in) old age. People who perpetuate this idea should spend one day doing what they love most, and then reflect on that time and see it as doing prayer.

Your prayer probably required more words when you were younger. I've discovered that aging can bring increased intuition. Prayer can be made of images, melodies, simple motions of the hands, even sighs and silence.

And creative work is a form of prayer; we are more likely to recognize this as the years go by. Many of us do have more time during the later seasons of life. And so as we paint, write, sculpt, take photographs, dance, or work higher mathematics, we can do devotions with a kind of calm and patience that we didn't know during earlier decades.

Your creative effort might simply be *looking*—not just reveling in towering red sunsets or shafts of sunlight coming through the redwoods, scenes you might see on a greeting card, but in anything God calls to your attention. It might be an ordinary black rock on the beach, lying with powerful presence in the sun; or a young swallow taking its first trial flight from under the eaves of your barn, while its parents call and swoop; or the painting of Jesus by William Blake, at the Fogg Art Museum in Cambridge, Massachusetts.

The prayer of the eye needs no words, because what you see dances straight through your whole brain and nervous system and imprints forever on memory and spiritual life. Aging people often find it easy to talk to God by gazing at icons, and I found out why in the ancient Church of Our Saviour at Karye, outside Istanbul, Turkey, where I saw the original mosaic of *Anastasis*, or resurrection. You've probably seen it in art books: Jesus, newly risen, is pulling Adam and Eve out of their tombs. Jesus is in gleaming white raiment; Adam and Eve have looks of shame that barely hide their secret surprise and delight. They'd dwelt for thousands of years in Sheol, where other souls were shadows and nothing moved; suddenly, Christ was there. After seeing that mosaic I knew something about God I hadn't known before.

Another time, I was lying on the dark forest floor, trying to shoot a picture of a wild calypso orchid that waved above a thick mat of moss. I nudged my macro lens to the right setting and was about to click when I noticed tiny white flowers on the moss, flowers that were invisible to the naked eye. They were so pearly, so perfect—and invisible except to one another—that I began to weep with awe at God's endless creativity.

Music, whether you make it or listen to it, is part of God's creative gift. You can be so aroused by the romantic sweeps of Ravel's *Daphnis and Chloe* or David Bowie's mandate to turn and face the strange, that you're transported, caught up to the third heaven—whether in the body or out of the body you may not know; God knows (2 Corinthians 12:2–4). I don't have to *think* prayer when I play my scratchy old recording of *Amahl and the Night Visitors.* Just hearing Melchoir's line "Swifter than lightning he shall soon dwell among us," and the mother's reply, "Oh, no, take back your gold. For such a king I've waited all my life!" still makes tears spring to my eyes (and I'm not a person who cries) and what's more important, sends me soaring toward the throne of God.

My eye, ear, and spirit are all awakened and turned toward heaven during Wagnerian operas and at art gallery openings where string quartets play Handel, and anytime they rerun the Christmas episode of *The West Wing*. The scene flicks back and forth between the president, listening to a children's choir—surrounded by poinsettias and candles and White House staff, dressed for Christmas—and the bleak Arlington honor-guard burial of a homeless veteran, attended only by the veteran's slow-minded brother, the president's secretary, and Toby, the White House communications officer. All on a bright, cold Christmas Day. At first, you only see the children's choir, singing "The Carol of the Drum" a cappella; but as the hearse pulls up in Arlington, the orchestra begins the relentless bass rum-tum-tum of the carol, and the children's voices turn into something like the Vienna Boys' Choir. Watching those five minutes of TV said more about God, and to God, than I could ever pray in words.

I was photographing Native American dancers at an Oregon powwow, had just moved my tripod, and was focusing my lens on a young Paiute man festooned with stiff black feathers and dancing alone in the center of the circle. I waited until he was leaning back, nearly doubled over backward and got ready to click my shutter, but a powwow official tapped me on the shoulder.

"Please don't take pictures of this," he said. "This is a prayer the dancer is doing. It's sacred."

I waited; and I was also doing prayer by standing still.

Sometimes, like the Paiute youth, I dance. I take my prayers through the slow dance of the Eucharist: kneeling, standing, genuflecting, making the sign of the cross. Sometimes I visit a more enthusiastic congregation and find myself doing a kind of ecstatic two-step. When my now-grown-up grandsons Andrew and Adam were little, we used to dance for Jesus under my sixteen hazelnut trees. We didn't spray the trees, so we let the nuts fall for the squirrels and bluejays; two-year-old Andrew sometimes would fling a handful of nuts while we danced. I had a little goat in the yard during those days, and she would leap into capriccios. Once Andrew's face lit up and he cried, "Gra'mother! I think I see Jesus dance too!"

You won't always like creating. Some days I would do anything to keep from writing. I'll even clean out cupboards or scrub my front gate. No one always enjoys the task; maybe that's why Dylan Thomas wrote that his craft was his sullen art. But he also said that he worked by singing light. The light, God, is singing: old age is an opera better than any written by Wagner, and we are only singing along with God, singing our designs and our equations and whatever else we create out of our hearts.

I create handmade paper and write poems on it. I take photographs of flowers and mushrooms and junkyards. I decorate my flower beds with ancient weathered bedsteads and broken birdhouses, and I refinish furniture. When I have time. None of these pursuits will make me rich or famous, but I am exercising the creative imperative that God thrust into me at my baptism, even if I don't do no fancy work.

CHAPTER TEN

How Shall
We Live, Now?

But this I call to mind,
and therefore I have hope:
The steadfast love of the LORD never ceases,
his mercies never come to an end.
Lamentations 3:21–22

A song every day. A song every day.
Rabbi Abraham Heschel

WE WHO ARE AGING WALK A TIGHTROPE, a line of tension between doing and not doing, between acting young or getting ready to die, between celebrating and preparing for infirmity. That tension is our human home; we have always lived in it whether or not we acquiesced to it or even paid any attention to it. You may be a commonsense person who just says you're here awhile, you do your best, and then you die.

Or you may be the more complicated sort who ponders each of life's vicissitudes. Regardless of your approach, you have to run along that tension the way bushy-tailed squirrels run across electrical and telephone wires.

And how shall we behave in that high-wire tension? We can shutter our souls as if we were already in the grave and pray for a happy death, or tiptoe toward risk with thudding hearts, or open ourselves to danger because—what the hell, we're not long for this life. We can choose parachute jumping and hang-gliding or dwell in the angst of old age, taking slow walks and gathering rosebuds while we may. But what does *God* want?

I think I heard the answer during a televised memorial service at the Washington National Cathedral just after the terrorist attacks on the World Trade Center and the Pentagon. The Reverend Billy Graham, that ancient lion who may have Parkinson's but shows no decrease in fervor, declared, "I've become an old man now, and I've preached all over the world, and the older I get, the more I cling to that hope that I started with many years ago and proclaimed in many languages to many parts of the world."

The hope I started with, he said. *The older I get, the more I cling to the hope.* His hope has always been that Christ will take him to heaven, hope that resurrection is a reality, and most of all, hope that he will endure to the end. That's it. From now until the time he dies, he plans to hope. And he's right; God designed us to live out hope. Sing hope, pray hope, talk hope, and do what we do every day with the hope of eternal life. Whether you're living in a nursing home or still working or running a 10K, do it filled with hope.

On the day of that disaster those of us who sat or stood like the men of Galilee on Ascension day, staring into heaven—this time not at the feet of the Lord as he disappeared into the cloud, but at the horror of a jet plane plunging into the nation's next-to-tallest buildings—must now decide to live with a hope that's good for the long haul. Perhaps now that our country has been struck with not only destruction but terror, we need that hope more than ever.

Cool, my inner critic wisecracks. *Sounds great.* But how does "living with hope" actually apply to peeling carrots or taking a bath or planting daffodils? I don't travel the world, preaching the gospel, like Billy Graham or Pope John Paul. How should we—not saints, just everyday struggling Christians—keep and exhibit our faith in Jesus' promises when we shop for clothes or use an ATM or sweep the front porch? And—what is harder—how do we face with hope the problems of aching bones and failing strength, the terror of the night, or the arrow that flies by day?

Hopefully, I mumble in response, feeling silly and inarticulate. *I'll live the rest of my life hopefully.* You don't know what I mean? Just imagine peeling carrots without hope or sweeping without hope. And then contrast that to the vision of doing it with delighted expectation. The difference is so clear, so obvious, that I—you—can affirm with Reverend Graham that we're clinging to hope. In fact we can pray hope, embrace the hope of eternal life, even when sorting the mail or driving a car. We can collect the evidence of God's action in our lives so that the hope within us grows like unborn children from this aging moment until the time when angels bear our souls away from earth.

To live hopefully is to live with delight. Delight in God's presence and in the expectation that you will one day see God face to face. And the less you trust the government or cosmetic manufacturers or long-term-care insurance to make your old age better, the greater your hope in God has to become. Hope can be, as it was for Emily Dickinson, "the thing with feathers / That perches in the soul / And sings the tune without the words / And never stops at all."

The Bible talks a lot about hope, saying "Be strong, and let your heart take courage, all you who wait for the Lord" (Psalm 31:24) and "For you, O Lord, are my hope, / my trust, O Lord, from my youth" (Psalm 71:5). But that is the hope that springs from *trust,* a hope based on the knowledge of God's action in human history. That's learned hope, taught hope, and recited hope. Old people want something more; we want the kind of hope that doesn't require knowledge or a sermon or reading, hope that will carry us until the day we enter God's presence either through death or because the angel has blown his trumpet while earth's elements melt away at the sight of Christ returned. And hope can't come from any source outside ourselves; hope originates inside, springing from faith and a belief that God's going to win. We have to create hope within, nurturing it until it finally begins to run on its own.

A Life of Expectation

We live within God's promises. "I have broken the bars of your yoke and made you walk erect," God said to the Israelites three thousand years ago (Leviticus 26:13). God is *for* us, urging us forward, saying, "Come on, you're clear," or "Don't step there: that's sin, a land mine. You're in danger. Walk over here." God is not only for us but with us, in the person of Christ leading us toward heaven and as the Holy Spirit setting us on holy fire. Everything good we do or think or want is a feeble reflection of God's doings and thoughts and desires.

Our proof of God's bias toward us is in God the Martyr, sacrificed in order that we can live. Christ became the Victim who is also the Victor over death and over our condemnation. Aquinas said it: *O salutaris hostia, quae caeli pandis osmium* . . . "O saving victim, opening wide the gate of heaven to man below." God the Victim, God the Crucified, God the Christ on the Cross threw himself into the breach for us; Jesus Christ the God-Man took sin upon himself and died as the perfect offering. The *salutaris hostia,* God the Son, firms up the hope Billy Graham started with and clings to now. When Jesus groaned in agony at

Gethsemane, hope sang its song. When the nails were hammered in, hope echoed through the world. And when Christ's blood fell from his wounds onto the earth, hope sprang up from the droplets. The flowers of hope.

How do we live, however many years we have left, in response to that sacrifice? *Hopefully,* we said. But now, God is asking for more. St. Anselm said it a few centuries ago, "He became what we were so that we might become what he is." Our life assignment is to become Christ.

Jesus talks about how we can participate in what that means. "If any want to become my followers, let them deny themselves and take up their cross and follow me. For those who want to save their life will lose it, and those who lose their life for my sake, and for the sake of the gospel, will save it."

Is all this something we can understand? Maybe. But it's not always easy to conform to. We "follow"—we go where Jesus goes—at least up to a point. But then we may discover that denying oneself means becoming humble in the eyes of God. It means making sure we don't determine our own destinies as disciples but follow the destiny God is shaping for each life. That independent man or woman within us has to decrease, and in this age of self-fulfillment, that doesn't come easy.

What if you can't lift your cross and follow? What if it is too heavy, too weighted down by your depression or your fear or your sin? Then Jesus does it for you, gives up being God and steps down to earth. When you can't lift your cross, he raises his like a standard, always ahead of you, with his face set toward Calvary.

Because none of us follow very well, he puts us on his shoulders like lost sheep and carries us home. And because we are sometimes sinners not worthy to be anywhere but hell, Jesus goes down there and cleans the place out. Our story is not only about suffering: the whole Bible is the story of God's mercy. St. Paul wrote to the Romans what is probably the most important statement ever written about our relationship with God: "For I am convinced that neither death, nor life, nor angels, nor rulers, nor things present, nor things to come, nor powers, nor height, nor depth, nor anything else in all creation, will be able to separate us from the love of God in Christ Jesus our Lord" (8:38–39).

So we can live hopefully. The flogging, the abuse, the trip to Golgotha, the crucifixion—they offer us salvation; the resurrection gives us hope. Whatever God demands of us, Jesus does for us and with us and in us.

Chuck Colson, the Watergate figure and founder of
Prison Fellowship, visited a prison in Brazil that is oper-
ated by Christians and founded on Christian principles.
This is what he found, as described in an article he wrote
years ago:

> *When I visited this prison, I found the*
> *inmates smiling, particularly the murderer*
> *who opened the gates and let me in.*
> *Wherever I walked, I saw men at peace. I*
> *saw clean living areas, people working*
> *hard. The walls were decorated with biblical*
> *sayings from Psalms and Proverbs. My*
> *guide escorted me to the notorious prison cell*
> *once used for torture. Today, he told me, that*
> *area houses only a single inmate. As we*
> *reached that cell, he paused and asked, "Are*
> *you sure you want to go in?"*
>
> *"Of course," I replied impatiently. "I've*
> *been in isolation cells all over the world."*
> *Slowly the guide swung open the massive*
> *door and I saw the prisoner in that punish-*
> *ment cell: a crucifix, beautifully carved by*

*the inmates—the prisoner Jesus, hanging on
a cross. The guide said softly, "He's doing
time for the rest of us."*

A Celebration Life

So the first steps in continuing with life after facing old
age and death are to bow to Christ's sacrifice, embrace
hope, and decide to live a celebration life. Whether
you're assembling your clothes in the morning or preparing a dinner or opening a new novel as you lie down at
night, celebrate. To live a celebration life is to live with
hope. Celebrate your life and God's life so the flames of
your spirit leap out to lighten and warm all life around
you, including the people who walk on your same path,
the ones who stand in line at the bank or sit near you in
restaurants and church, because you can send out waves
of God's love. The smile of a celebration person is different from that of someone who thinks life is a burden.
And if your spirit is dancing, the people you encounter
will hear the music.

St. Paul said, "Rejoice always, pray without ceasing, give thanks in all circumstances; for this is the will of God in Christ Jesus for you" (1 Thessalonians 5:16–18). The will of Christ is that we dance and sing and pray and learn gratitude. So look out between the slats of your bedroom miniblinds when you wake, and thank God, who set light in motion to create and occupy creation. You offer your spirit to God in the sense of returning home: if God made you out of dust from the fiery stars, embrace that fire to be purified and renewed. And God will be present with you, as will angels in festal garments.

Remember that you were not an afterthought. In that first nanosecond of creation, when fire erupted and the explosion caused life to form, you were present in God's mind, present as a baby, as a child, as a young man or woman, maybe as a parent, and as an aging child of God. You are made of the dust of the stars that rose out of that original fireball; you are a stage in God's invention of matter. Sometime during the last 12 billion years, God thought something like, "I'm going to make stars, planets, space, soil, bugs, ice, granite, ducks, kangaroos, redwoods, and people." And because God's thoughts are commands, the universe happened. First nothing, then everything. Matthew Fox says that when you go outside to look at the stars, you're searching for your ancestors.

If we are to celebrate as we age, then we have to learn awe for the universe and all its creatures. The aim of such awe is that nobody will ever again be guilty of wanton waste of our planet's resources, never commit violence toward humans, other animals, or the earth. Remembering that we and they were formed from the same elements—and, in a sense, at the same moment— we'd better pray that other people are also burning with the light that God spoke into being. If we block that light by polluting or killing or hating, then we are responsible for darkness in the earth. And I don't have time at my age to entertain the dark. I might live another year or twenty, but I don't have any guarantees, and I don't know how long I'll be energetic or able to battle with evil. So I have to live for the good, celebrate the good, *become* the good. I am pressed to live as the encourager and the helper. Maybe you can retire from your job, but you can never quit working for good. Even if you're so decrepit you can't move, you can still pray.

We live with hope, and we celebrate. We revere our world, and finally, we do good. That is the assignment God gives us. We have those four tasks, and it behooves us to do them. And if we fail? Our failure was crucified with Christ and will not be held against us, but I think we still have to try. Could God fail? Well, that's downright silly. I once read a novel in which the angels could not work because people didn't pray. When did the angels fall under our jurisdiction? They're God's servants, not ours. And saying that angels have to be supported by our prayers is like Peter Pan, watching Tinkerbell's light fade away, saying, "Oh, please! Clap if you believe in fairies."

God never slips, never falls, never fails. Yes, God the Son was crucified, but that was not failure. Do you think he could not have appealed to his Father, who would have at once sent him more than twelve legions of angels? And the fact that God cannot fail gives me hope, and hope is where I started this chapter. Hope aspires to a goal, and the goal is God; and while I am running toward God, I also live in this world and have opportunities for love and fun and profound thought. And God has made it clear that the purpose of life is to live, not to simply wait for death. Living a hopeful life doesn't have to mean relentless cheerfulness in the face of disaster. I'll never forget the day when I was unloading my groceries and knocked a full gallon of vegetable oil to the kitchen floor. Because that house was built on a cement slab, the floors were hard as marble, so oil and shards of glass covered the kitchen. My neighbor, a constantly sunny woman who had accompanied me to the market, sat on the couch in the living room and through the archway watched me struggle. When I slipped, cut myself, and finally muttered some unprintable words, she smiled and shook her finger, saying, "Now, now! Say, 'Praise the Lord' and rejoice in all things."

Her constant red-robin cheeriness had irritated me for years; just then I found it unbearable (and so was cleaning up the mess with absolutely no help from her; she just sat and watched). I think it was a week before that floor was completely free of oil slicks; the time it took to get over my neighbor's lack of sensitivity was longer.

Neither does being hopeful mean that you go around constantly surly or gloomy. You don't have to be a comedian, but you do have to look expectant, as if you would consider that good things are possible. The trick is not how to look, but how to be; maybe for Hamlet all the world was a stage, but for us here on the planet, the drama is a real one: God's documentary on human life.

Can you have hope when your right arm is near crippled with arthritis, or when you spend some of your best waking hours at the dentist, or while your neighbor is dying of cancer and ignorant armies clash by night on the darkling plain? Well, you can keen with misery or live in terror or hate everything; or you can, like Billy Graham, cling to the hope you started with. God is whispering to you right now to hope, to celebrate; please, please have enough faith to think that maybe after all, the best is yet to come.

PART III

Steps in the Journey

❦

My foot has held fast to his steps;
I have kept his way and have not turned aside.

Job 23:11

CHAPTER ELEVEN

Friends and Counselors

I do not call you servants any longer, because the
servant does not know what the master is doing;
but I have called you friends, because I have made
known to you everything that I have heard
from my Father.

John 15:15

Love's mysteries in soules doe grow.

John Donne

MAYBE THE HARDEST CONCEPT FOR ANY of us to drape around our lives is "community." We love the idea but may shy away from the reality of it. A real community—the church, a study club or social circle, the gym or the neighborhood—has people in it. People! People with bad habits and worse dispositions, people who are too loud or too silent or who control and manipulate, moody folks who are never the same from one day to the next; people, indeed, who go into our bathrooms and snoop in our medicine cabinets or who are rude to our children or snippy about two blades of our grass creeping over their property lines. Community would be fine—if it weren't for the people. Yet those people are necessary for Christian life because the place in which we see God face to face is in the Eucharist, and Eucharist involves the community of the church.

How We Define Community

When a community is small enough, we call it friendship. Three women who meet for Bible study, four guys who drink coffee at Wal-Mart every morning. Or maybe community is just one more person, a walking or jogging companion. Of course, friendship can be mysterious and not always easy.

How does community change as we age? And why? Maybe we become friends because we are all one—one blood, one human genome—and we see ourselves in one another. We hold in limbic memory a time when we had to cling together because we had common enemies: fierce animals, warring tribes, famine, or the threat of plague or fevers or fatal boils. And the greatest reason of all for friendship is that God said, "It is not good for the man to live alone; I will make him a helper as his partner."

Notice that God didn't say it was bad for the human to live without reproducing or without sex or without someone to fix supper. When God said, "I will make him a helper as his partner," the Hebrew word translated as "helper" is the same one often used to describe God in Scripture, as in "I shall again praise him, / my help and my God" (Psalm 43:5). God knew we also needed flesh-and-blood helpers who would be part of our lives, so God created marriage and friendship. It really isn't good for the *adam*—the human—to be alone, no matter how natural solitude feels.

Just a step outside community are our enemies. We sometimes form groups to defend ourselves against someone we think wants to harm us. Citizens of Israel draw together because they're certain that Palestinians mean harm, and vice versa. We in the United States became as one in our prosecution of the war against Al Qaeda, in the same way we pulled together during World War II.

I am not a "needy" person; I rarely feel desperate for someone to talk to. I'm perfectly happy alone most of the time, reading, writing, listening to music, or planting violets in my yard. So I have to try harder to make friends, because I could wake up someday and realize that I'm all alone: maybe crippled by a stroke and with no friends to visit me or who care if I live. *It is not good for the man* [or woman] *to live alone.* So introverts, listen up: it's fun to be by yourself, but you need to cultivate the love of other people.

When I teach or preach or speak, I become outgoing and effusive, perfumed by the fragrance of my own goodness, expansive and generous, able to remain on aching feet to answer a few more questions. I crack jokes, wave my arms, and become funnier than I am when I write. The hard part is when I have to stand at the back of the room afterward, shaking hands and finding humble replies to too much praise. Because then I have to relate to people instead of just entertaining them, have to relate to them and care about what they're saying. Who they are has to matter to me. I thrive on being alone—in fact, I need to be alone a great deal, not only to write but to restore my energy. Being social doesn't come naturally to me—maybe it doesn't to you either. But life calls me out of my cave, and my aging—the oldness of my body, the

sense in my spirit that time is passing—reminds me that
I can't face the future alone. I have to seek community.

How to Do Community Better

Somebody needs to tell me—and all of us—how to do
community better. We have marriage and parenting and
family counseling, but how many psychologists advertise
friendship therapy? Jesus called us his friends, but it's all
too easy to love Jesus and dislike all his other friends.
This needs fixing if the human race is to survive any
longer. We have to start warming up all relationships,
personal, political, and international if humankind is
going to continue. But there isn't a set of steps we can
take to have decent relationships. Thomas Moore said,
in his introduction to *Soul Mates,* that the human heart
is a mystery in the religious sense; the heart, he says, is
unfathomable, beyond manipulation, with the traces of
God's finger showing.

"Yet in our time," he says, "we have tried to apply the
same kind of mechanical and structural thinking that has
made an astounding technological world. We regard
marriage and families and speak of systems, and we try

to help people 'relate' to each other by organizing groups and developing exercises for communication and intimacy." He's saying that friendship and community belong in the sphere of creativity and imagination, like fireflies and diamonds and kabuki dancing.

But while theories about community are fine, putting them to use can feel close to impossible. We may get trapped, suspended somewhere between the need for friends and the need to be alone. And we can't just hang onto either our children or our relatives and say that we live in community. We need special friends, counselors, fellow travelers. And for some reason, much of society thinks that we want to spend the rest of our lives in the exclusive company of people our own age. So we have gated over-fifty-five housing communities, where no child's voice is heard, where no mothers stand in the street yelling for kids to come in for dinner. And society has built us senior centers and offered us a kind of aging limbo where we smile, nod, and learn to do crafts.

I for one never want to live where I can't hear kids playing, and I would not like to spend all my friendship hours with men and women my age. So I have Jo and Maron, of my generation, and Kathy, Linda, and Debbie, who are younger. Three of us are spiritual directors, the last three writers, all of us Christians. I have never seen all six of these women in the same place, and I don't know how much they would enjoy one another if I did invite them together to, say, tea and scones at my house. They are five women between forty and sixty-five, and I love them.

As I write this I wonder if they know I love them, and I vow to make an inventory of my manners. Have I actually said, "I love you" to each of them? I wonder if my demeanor with them stays warm and affectionate or whether I show off how brittle and sarcastic I can be. I know that when I found out that *sarcasm* literally means "tearing of the flesh," I began to watch my mouth. I love to be funny, but that little sting might be actually ripping up a friend. I take my friends' advice much of the time. When Maron tells me to read something or pray some way, I do it. When Jo offers me a book or videotape, I read or watch it. When the other writers tell me what to do about my work, I listen because I trust them.

How to Tell a Friend
from an Alligator

I don't trust everyone, partly because I've found out that some people are not friends, but alligators. I learned this from my grandson Andrew, when he was about three. We were driving to my house, I at the wheel and he in his car seat in the back. He made up a song as we rolled along, a song about trees, clouds, and birds, and the motorbike he could hear behind us.

Suddenly he shouted, "Gra'mother!"

"Yes, Andrew?"

"Gra'mother, a dog is a *friend!*" he announced in a delighted voice, and I agreed that yes, a dog was indeed a friend.

We rode another mile, and he called out, "Gra'mother! Gra'mother, a *cat* is a friend!"

I said yes, that a cat was a friend. Just as I was finally pulling into our cul-de-sac, he said sadly, "Gra'mother? Gra'mother, I don't think an alligator is a friend."

An alligator *isn't* a friend. I could keep one in my bathtub and feed it every day for a year, sing it songs, and stroke its knobby forehead—and it would still try to take my hand off if it was hungry or annoyed. And as we age, we sometimes get careless with alligators.

Most people can tell a friend from an alligator, but I have at least one acquaintance who never could and who gets worse every year. Pat is sixty-five, a widow who is lonely and leaps into friendships without checking for species or disposition. Pretty soon she's limping back, bleeding and nearly dead from the bites she's received. And I know she isn't alone; aging people can get desperate for friendship. The spouse may have died or gone off with a trophy wife or a lifeguard. And even some spouses can become alligators, especially as they age. What was a tendency to be a teeny bit self-centered or jealous or devious in youth can mature into powerful jaws, strong teeth, and a thick, checkered hide.

Some old friends who are also aging can, because of their life circumstances or hormone loss or brain changes, suddenly turn reptilian. And nobody can wound you like a friend; the hurt when someone you love turns and whips you with a scaled tail is overwhelming. Even David said, "It is not enemies who taunt me— / I could bear that; / it is not adversaries who deal insolently with me— / I could hide from them. / But it is you, my equal, / my companion, my familiar friend, / with whom I kept pleasant company; / we walked in the house of God with the throng" (Psalm 55:12–13).

I've endured some bites and always from a cleverly disguised alligator dressed as a woman at church or a writing buddy or a fawning student. Unlike Pat, I have devised an alligator-detection system that works most of the time, although I've sustained a few scars. I'm sorry to say, in the middle of all this spiritual stuff, that they're out there, people who can hurt you or betray you or even ruin your family or business. They can't help it: an alligator is, after all, just an alligator—but never a friend.

Alligators bite. They can take off a hand or even cause death, and you've got to know the difference between friends and these reptiles. A good friendship is however *you* define it, but learn to avoid "impulse buying." If you're a friend to someone but not friends with him or her, you may be in gator country. Some alligators are so empty inside that they gobble everything, trying to get full. Which they never do. So unless you're just befriending someone for the sake of Christ, expect to do as much receiving as you do giving, because an empty, grasping alligator has nothing to give you.

Some alligators want to star. Like Gertrude Lawrence's character Liza Elliott in the musical *Lady in the Dark*, if there's a party they want to be the host of it; if there's a town they have to be the toast of it, with an adoring audience of scientific, artistic notables. They have to be the center of every conversation, the shining nexus of any group, and they welcome your friendship; you're one more worshipper in their church of self. They can make you believe that you're part of their inner circle, but in the end, you'll notice that you're part of a large group. And you're bleeding.

There are borrowing alligators who never pay back anything, whether you lend them a cup of sugar or a thousand dollars, so keep your antennas up after the first loan. Slippery alligators appear to want friends, but they always slither away and leave you wondering what you did wrong. They hate intimacy, so watch your new friends to see if they glide away from people when they get too close. And of course alcoholic or substance-abuse alligators who won't give up booze or drugs may steal from you, harm you physically, damage your property, or ruin your reputation. If you detect alcohol on your pal's breath too often, or too many changes in his or her personality and behavior, you can't come to the rescue. Be part of an intervention if you like, but begin backing off as soon as you're sure something is wrong in the substance department.

How You Create Community

Where do you meet new friends when your best pal has died or moved across the country, when you have no spouse, and you don't play bridge? The art of friendship and the places you meet people don't change after age fifty or seventy or even ninety. You meet them in church, in line at the supermarket, while walking dogs, or knocking on a neighbor's door. You find new friends in a writing class or at a seminar on insurance. You don't have to look for someone of a particular age or gender; one of my friends is a high-school-aged writer who saw me editing a manuscript in McDonald's and got up the nerve to come talk to me. Another is a man about eighty whom I met at a conference.

What does all this have to do with spiritual life during our later years? God wants to glorify everyone and make them part of the great gathering of the elect. The question is what everyone's connection is to *individual* spiritual life (not counting spiritual directors and pastors and nuns and such folk; we usually have at least an idea of what their relationship is to the numinous). Why do we need one another anyway?

Need is a nondescript word, and *needy* is now thrown about in conversation and diagnoses the way *inferiority complex* was when I was a kid. When I say that we need one another, I mean that we have interlocking shapes that must fit together if we are to form a greater whole. C. S. Lewis said that when God looks at humanity, we appear less as separate dots and more like a tree. Or perhaps we're like a spiral galaxy, with our swirling outer arms outstretched to embrace Christ's knees. Although every star is discrete, disconnected from the others when you are on it or near it, the galaxy looks more like a lacy whole, a handful of light with no separations in it. I'm joined to my nice neighbor who paints her house an awful mustard yellow and also to my less-pleasant, negative neighbor whose house and yard are, oddly enough, a delight to my eye. I'm connected to the people in my congregation, the ones I admire and the ones I'd honestly rather sidestep than talk to. I can't be friends with alligators, but I have to recognize that Jesus died to give them life, and we're joined together.

And this whole tree of us is a continuous opportunity to love one another and love God. Christians are more than a tree; we are connected to one another by the shed blood of Jesus Christ. We are a branch of that tree, a branch that can bear fruit; and the profound mystery of that bearing is that we have to do it together. While I am writing this book, you are preparing a meal or driving a school bus or programming a computer, and we are bearing fruit separately, but God sees us and our work as one heavy, dark bunch of grapes. When we come together to make Eucharist on Sunday morning, we bear fruit together. And if one of us falls down and can't get up, we've all fallen; so we need one another's support.

Over the years we've seen a lot of "we are all one" campaigns, but most of them were sentiment and had nothing to do with reality. However, when we sing "One bread, one body," we've got to mean it for everyone in the congregation and diocese and church and planet. Some days, I don't mean it. Over the years I've said many words and sung all kinds of songs about all men and woman being brothers and sisters, about "in your body, Lord, we are one," about "here we are, all together as we sing our song"—while nurturing a strong feeling of dislike for the man sitting in front of me. Though he has hurt and offended me over and over, I've got to pray for my enemy and do nice things for him; send him a birthday card, pray for him every day, draw him into fellowship, and try to see him as God sees him. Only with the help of God can I learn to relate better, love others, and act out the unity that Jesus, on the night he was betrayed, prayed for us to have. I can do this only with the help of God, because I have to learn to see with God's eyes and love with God's heart.

Even if I never accomplish that kind of relationship perfection, my own intimate circle of people has to deliver God's word or spirit to me, hold me up if my knees buckle or my mind goes on a walkabout. The older I get, the more I need the company of others on the journey, some who are ahead, others who are nearby, and yet others who are younger and still strong and hopeful; and they need me.

Will we meet in heaven? On the day of the resurrection, when we are restored in immortal, incorruptible bodies, will we see one another and rush to offer our love and greetings? I don't know. I suspect that once I see God, nothing else will capture my attention. But I hope everyone will wave anyway, because maybe the old saw that love is eternal might turn out to be true.

John Donne's old command not to send to find for whom the bell tolls is apt. He knew. We are one another's goodness and sin and success and failure. We share the common fate of death and the common offer of God's grace. Maybe if we join hands, if we have coffee or talk to strangers on airplanes or play games together, we can climb up the mountain of aging with wit and goodness. Because we need companions on the way.

CHAPTER TWELVE

Cleaning Out
the Heart

*For if you forgive others their trespasses, your
heavenly Father will also forgive you.*

Matthew 6:14

*Forgiveness breaks the chain of causality because he
who forgives you—out of love—takes upon himself
the consequences of what you have done.
Forgiveness, therefore, always entails a sacrifice.*

Dag Hammarskjöld, *Markings*

I WAS AT A RETREAT CENTER IN THE ROCKIES,
giving a workshop on forgiveness, when a gentle,
soft-voiced woman asked how she could bless and
release the man who had hurt her son even though that
person was unknown to her. "Did the individual molest
him?" I asked, getting my ammunition ready. She could,

I was going to say, begin to heal her son's and her own hurt—.

"Killed him," she said. "Stabbed him and left him on the sidewalk to die."

Suddenly, I had nothing to say. All my theories about forgiveness were ineffectual and fatuous. I was teaching forgiveness, although nothing so bad had ever happened to me or to anyone I love. Forgiveness for that woman, who had lost her only child to a faceless assailant, may take years. Death was the unarguable element in the situation, and it won, because the first person that grieving woman had to forgive was God—and I didn't know if she could, not at that point.

After I got home from the conference, I started thinking and making notes about forgiveness. The first step may be confronting God, and if you're aging, you don't have a long time to get around to that. Deep down, behind many breastbones and maybe lurking in back of every spleen, is the belief that God is the wizard behind the curtain. Faced with unbearable pain, you might convince yourself that God is not only responsible for everything that happens to you but also ultimately unfair.

Anger at God

God is not fair; God is just, and in the Bible, justice isn't about executing killers and locking up drug dealers up for life. Old Testament justice is more like what we now call charity. God's justice includes being gracious to the undeserving; Luke 6:35 tells us that the "Most High . . . is kind to the ungrateful and the wicked"—including murderers who stab young men and leave them on the sidewalk to die.

And I know how you feel. Just as I convince myself not to blame God, I get news that makes me sick. Today was a wonderful day: nothing is more beautiful than spring in Oregon, with the bright green hillsides and the air heavy with lilac. We drove seventy miles south, hoping to find a nursery that sold a certain native tree, and though we didn't find one, we enjoyed the scenery. We ate in a Mexican restaurant on the way home and raved about the bright blue ceanothus, or "mountain lilac," on the hillsides. Even the dog looked rested and jubilant as he climbed out of the car onto our driveway.

I strolled into my office to check my e-mail and found the message that one of my best friends, another Christian writer, a woman with a beautiful spirit who has supported and encouraged a bipolar husband for forty years, had gone to the hospital for gall bladder surgery. But she's going home because she has cancer of the liver, kidney, and pancreas.

I felt like President Bartlett in the *West Wing* episode in which his longtime secretary was killed in her new car. Bartlett, played by Martin Sheen, stood in front of the altar at the Washington National Cathedral, looked at the altar, and said, "You're a son-of-a-bitch, God."

Yeah, I said. *You're everything I was afraid you might be: a monster, a villain who made us for your sadistic pleasure. You're nothing but a giant maw, a sucking mouth that consumes us, snatches up and devours everyone, licking its lips. You're always looking for something to lap up—a deer impaled on barbed wire, a frail pink orchard beaten to death by hail, a woman who loves life only to be gobbled by cancer.*

Just after telling my readers to make peace with God, I turned on the Almighty with such venom that it rose up in my throat. And then I sat down in my darkened office and let sadness consume me. I called my friend Linda, who also loves my sick friend.

But even in my grief I have to admit that God isn't the trickster who orchestrates human events behind that curtain. Pain and evil occur just because they do, and Jesus reminded us that we'll have trouble while we're on earth. So children get cancer and cystic fibrosis and neurological diseases while others die on the sidewalk from knife wounds, not because God wills sorrow but because they—we—live in a world where genes go awry and so do personalities. Hurricanes destroy houses on the Florida coast because people built there of their own volition, not because God told them to. My friend probably has cancer because her mother and grandmother did; in fact, she's had a longer life than they did.

This free will thing is what's wrong with earth. If everything were just up to God, if we didn't have to constantly make choices and hope they're right, in fact, if we didn't make so many *wrong* choices, then life would be, well, easier, if nothing else. The world is not only imperfect, it wasn't even perfected by the Resurrection: we have to live out Christ's command to become perfect as our Father in heaven is perfect—the Father who then hands us free will. The world is full of sadness and terror, and "every day's trouble is enough for today." The hero of *A Farewell to Arms* says on the last page, "They don't tell you the rules, and then they expect you to do the right thing." Of course, God *has* told us the rules, and the right thing—the only thing—is to grab onto Christ's coattails and slide into heaven while you grip them. Because free will alone makes us too likely to do the wrong thing.

Every human being has at least one enemy or has been the victim of someone; you probably haven't lost a child to a murderer, but you have suffered too, and pain is pain. Your hatred of someone may have colored your life for years. Nevertheless, the one thing you don't want to drag into the last part of your life is that garbage bag full of grudges and hurts you've saved up, including that resentment toward God.

The Damage of Bitterness

Unforgiveness can kill you, can make you rigid clear to your arteries, and can clog your creativity forever. You may not always remember the connection between your deep, hidden emotions and your physical body, but the link is there, and you probably have as many health problems as the number of people you still haven't forgiven.

I know a woman who has devoted her life to hating her former husband. He was indeed a bad mate: he was unfaithful, he drank to excess, he abused her physically, and finally he molested and injured their young daughter. She was justified when she left him and made sure he could never again be alone with the little girl. She was justified when she pressed charges and saw him go to jail. But she didn't seek healing; she sought revenge. His going to jail and the loss of his position as a stockbroker weren't enough.

She ate, drank, and bathed in her hatred. She often called his mother, his boss, and several of his friends to harangue them about their guilt in making the man become evil. When he got out of prison and went to work at a laundry for minimum wage, she harassed court clerks, trying to raise the amount of alimony and child support he paid. She quit her part-time job so she could spend her days either on the telephone, screaming at the husband and his coworkers, or writing letters to his parents or the courts.

After a year of this, he disappeared, ditching his child-support payments. Then she really put her hatred into gear, and has spent the last twenty years searching for him, depriving her daughter of attention, love, and even a college education because she spent all her time—and her inheritance from her father—on private detectives.

She has no friends now, and the daughter she saved from her husband is estranged from her mother. The aging woman lives a lonely, impoverished life and blames her husband for her state. She doesn't realize that she is the one who wrecked her present existence. When anyone tells her she could be happier if she forgave her ex-husband, she recites his sins, thinking that to forgive would somehow excuse his behavior.

You have to forgive your parents and siblings and schoolmates for the ways they made your childhood miserable, if they did. You have to forgive the teacher who, after you worked for a week on your report, accused you of cheating. Or the stepfather who whacked you so hard you wanted to kill him. You have to forgive the thief who stole your wallet and ran your credit cards up, as well as the doctor that did you more harm than good. The more unjustly someone treated you, the more powerful God's command for you to forgive.

Forgiveness isn't just "nice"; it's necessary for your salvation. Jesus said in his Sermon on the Mount, "If you do not forgive others, neither will your Father forgive your trespasses." You won't receive God's pardon until you forgive not only the people who did you wrong, but even the evils done to the world by terrorists and child molesters and murderers. Without forgiving, you're unforgiven and might be headed to hell if you don't seek forgiveness from God. And after a certain age, you can't afford to be in that condition: you're on borrowed time as it is.

Relinquishing the memory of terrible injustice, mistreatment, or offense can take you into shalom country. Forget about fairness and justice and being right. Let go of your rage toward the uncle who left his estate to your brother, and the anger you feel toward your brother. If your neighbor's trashy yard gets your goat, forgive him, and if you're still mad at the brutal way your father treated you, ask God to help you let it go.

Stop telling yourself the stories over and over again, and quit reaffirming that you have a right to be mad. Since God gave you free will, you have the "right" to hold onto bitterness, but your rights are killing you, making you older faster, and robbing you of health. Your right to withhold forgiveness can keep you from perfect peace.

Our Confusion about Forgiveness

Be careful not to confuse forgiveness with condoning the evil someone has done. Neither is forgiveness merely coming to an understanding or an explanation of someone's actions; you can forgive without excusing. Saying that Uncle Henry was sick and distraught when he swore at your child is not forgiving: it's excusing. And you would be wrong to condone what God wants to redeem. Suicide bombers, rapists, and petty shoplifters are all sinners, and you can't say that what they did was all right; you can only forgive them for their sin.

There's nothing natural about forgiveness. Wild animals that rip one another apart do not remit one another's sins. The woman might forgive her son's murderer but it wouldn't be considered "normal." But beyond natural and normal lies God's country, where earthly values are upside down, where vengeance and fairness have no foothold. I'll never understand, nor condone, rapists or suicide bombers or people who kidnap for ransom. What they do is wrong, wrong, wrong, and nothing can undo that. But I can say, as God does to me, "I have blotted out your iniquity."

The Benefit of Forgetting

And then you have to forget the evil act. The writer Sholem Asch said, "Not the power to remember, but its very opposite, the power to forget, is a necessary condition for our existence." You must beg God to help you forget the sinner's incursion into your peace. And while forgetting isn't easy, God commanded that you do it. And God does it "as far as the east is from the west, so far he removes our transgressions from us" (Psalm 103:12).

Yes, God forgets. Every time you ask to be forgiven, whether for a small sin like trying to elude your needy, tiresome neighbor by going around the block for the bus, or for a big abomination like adultery, you wipe the slate clean and God forgets about it.

Sometimes you think you've forgiven, even tried hard to forget, but you have a little something leftover.

Once I was driving to a meeting a hundred miles away, listening to a Christian program on the car radio. A pastor spoke about the reasons for unforgiveness and offered a quick fix for every one of them. None of them applied to my problem; I'd been mad at one of my parents for forty years. More, I guess, because our history went back to my childhood, and nothing had ever changed.

So I switched off the radio and for the thousandth time asked God to help me forgive my parent. And as usual, I had a tiny knot of something remaining, something that pressed against my breastbone.

"What is it?" I asked God, and the answer was swift.

"Resentment," God said. "You're keeping a kernel of resentment."

"But why? I *want* to forgive."

"You're using anger as an anesthetic for pain," God said.

Whoa. When God convicts, God doesn't fool around. I prayed the rest of the way to Portland, asking the Almighty to show me what to do. After the meeting I skipped the luncheon, picked up a fast-food taco, and headed home. I was hardly able to choke down the food, because I was crying so hard, forcing myself to feel my pain.

The next day was Ash Wednesday. Without much sense of sacrament or ritual, I tried to offer up anger and resentment. I didn't realize how completely I would have to face the agony of my childhood, or I might have retreated. But I took a vow and so all during Lent I set aside some time every day to relive a scene in which my parent mistreated or hurt me. But this time, instead of getting angry, I forced myself to experience my sorrow, and I cried. I think I shed more tears during that forty days than in the ten years before them. And I said kind words to myself: "It's all right, honey," words my parents should have said to soothe my tears but didn't.

I went through that process until Easter morning, when I woke up and thanked God for resurrecting me— and my childhood memories. I was at more peace than I had ever been in my life, and that day I began to feel younger, stronger, more like—like myself. And on that day I wrote the word *shalom* in my journal.

Now I'm going to try hard to forgive God and the world for my friend who is so sick. Why forgive? First, because we're commanded to do so. Second, because we're reminded that we will be forgiven in the same exact measure we use to remit others' sins.

Third, forgiveness eases aging. We feel better and act a lot better when we aren't lugging the unforgiven sins of other people with us. And finally, because forgiveness is a mysterious, mystical event whereby we "put on Christ" and let God give us flesh-and-blood hearts instead of stone.

CHAPTER THIRTEEN

To Follow Thee More Nearly

Then Jesus said to the Jews who had believed in
him, "If you continue in my word, you are truly my
disciples; and you will know the truth, and the
truth will make you free."
John 8:31–32

Day by day, day by day,
Of thee, dear Lord, three things we pray:
to love thee more dearly, see thee more clearly,
Follow thee more nearly,
Day by Day.
St. Richard of Chichester

B ECOMING A TRUE FOLLOWER OF CHRIST IS A
process, one that now, in old age, we need to refine.
We're getting ready, after all, for the glory road. No
longer content with blind faith or childhood faith, or any

kind of religious practice that doesn't take us closer to Christ, we've started reaching for more: not only to have more, but to be and do more.

I take my example from my dog, a fourteen-year-old Shih Tzu, Tai-Pan. He is remarkably energetic and resilient, bounding through the house or down to the mailbox with me as if he were a puppy. He is my constant companion, and wherever I go, he goes. The hardest moment of his life is Sunday morning, when I leave him behind and go to church, because on most other car trips I take him along. When I get home, he dances, turns circles, and barks with delight.

He sleeps by my desk while I work, curls up beside me when I read or watch TV, lies on my stomach while I read in bed (occasionally pushing over the book so he can see my face), and he sleeps in the curve of my knees. He sometimes sits at my feet, looking up at me in adoration. To him, I am God, providing food, love, comfort, and safety, and he is my faithful follower.

To be Christ's follower, Christ's disciple, means to offer him the trust and adoration my little dog offers me. The closer we get to the end of our lives, the more fealty is necessary in our faith. The "semper fidelis" of the Marine Corps has to be the aging man or woman's dedication to the Lord.

Belief for the Journey

Some churches have discipleship programs for new members, something beyond introductory classes. Most of them start with assigning a seasoned believer to mentor the new one. They study the Bible and participate in other activities and studies together, until the newer member feels able to fly on his or her own. I haven't made sufficient inquiries into these programs to know how well they work, but I admire their intent. The seasoned traveler knows which route to take through the mountain pass, which plants to eat along the way, and where to ford the river.

We can go to friends and counselors for guidance. But as we enter these later years, our guide has to be Christ himself. We aren't spiritual children any more; in fact, we are the older generation, the seasoned travelers. And we're packing for the journey. If you were making a list of necessary take-alongs for discipleship, the first would, of course, be belief.

I've talked about faith and belief before; in fact, I devoted a lot of the second chapter of this book to faith, but I have to reiterate that belief is so basic you may sometimes ignore whether you have it. You can't follow what you don't accept or have any confidence in: if you don't believe in a law you probably won't obey it, and if you refuse to accept that Jesus was the Son of God and rose from the dead, you probably won't obey him, either. Belief is not the same as faith, and it is not necessarily the same as understanding. Most of us believe that scientist Stephen Hawking's theories about quantum mechanics are right, but few people understand them well or at all. Belief in Christ is like that. A disciple isn't a theologian; a believer is one who looks to Jesus and says, like St. Thomas, "My Lord and my God."

Belief isn't always easy. Some days I wake up having decided, somewhere before I came back from my dreams and into my world, that my whole set of Christian beliefs is a myth and I'm not going for it any more. Fortunately, a cup of steaming, fresh-ground coffee almost always moves me closer to faith, and by midmorning God has usually restored me to true belief. Faith is a gift from God, but I have to pray constantly for belief.

Belief is based on knowledge and experience. I've walked on the hill of the Beatitudes in Israel, sat in a boat on the Sea of Galilee, and carried a cross up the Via Dolorosa in Jerusalem. I read *Biblical Archaeology* magazine, and I've devoured so much theology that I could probably pass the General Ordination Exams (not that I'm seeking ordination, of course). I believe, because I see enough evidence of the Bible's being revealed and of lives changed when people come to Christ. Belief is *my* job: God gave me five senses, a capacity for deep feeling, and a brain big enough to make the decision that God is and that Christ is Lord. So I pray for God to show me what I need to see and to help me believe.

But faith is God's department. Give God an ounce of belief and God will pour down a gallon of faith. My faith is rooted not in fact or experience, but in God's own being, and it resides not in my mind or senses or feelings, but in what Jesus always called "the heart." Belief is mental; faith is a spiritual gift that God offers to everyone. And even on those dark, gray mornings when my knees ache and I don't believe anything, I feel the dragonfly of faith fluttering deep, deep inside me. And faith restores my belief.

Trust in the One We Follow

The Gospel of Matthew says that one who endures to the end will be saved. Can we really hold onto belief, hold onto it through the changes of aging, beyond the aching bones or the failing vision? Can we endure the rest of our lives without letting pain or distress or poverty change our faith? I don't think we have much choice at this point. And if we do lose faith for a moment we must, like the prodigal, remember God's grace and come home to be reconciled. At some point we have to keep telling ourselves, *Hang on. Hang on. You're a disciple. Don't give up.*

And belief isn't all. A believing disciple of Jesus must, of course, trust him and respond without suspicion, anxiety, or insecurity. Abraham got no instructions about his mission or his final destination, but he got up and left Ur, and later he left Haran at God's command. The Virgin Mary didn't inquire of Gabriel as to the details of her Son's conception and birth. The early church martyrs had absolute confidence that they would go straight to God. Blessed Julian of Norwich trusted God's message that "All shall be well." And after sixty or seventy or more years on earth you've learned to trust Jesus Christ with your life; otherwise you could come to the end in terrible fear.

I trusted more earthly things when I was younger. I've learned to be suspicious: I am certain, for instance, that most mechanical devices, appliances, and put-together kits were invented to fox and frustrate me. I can't always count on instructions or recipes to be fool-proof. I frankly do not trust Congress to work innocently, with only the country's benefit as their aim. I don't trust airport employees to catch bad guys every time. I am edgy about the kitchen practices of many restaurants. God and God alone is worthy of trust.

After some of Jesus' followers deserted him, he asked the twelve, "Do you also wish to go away?" Simon Peter answered, "Lord, to whom can we go? *You* have the words of eternal life." *The words of eternal life,* which loomed more distantly when we were thirty, now hold tremendous import and tweak our grandest imagination. The words of eternal life are not an incantation that we can keep reciting, hoping we'll be muttering it on our deathbed so we can get past the pearly gates. The words of eternal life are the whole gospel and they are "Come, follow me."

Dietrich Bonhoeffer said in *The Cost of Discipleship* that when Jesus calls a man, he bids him come and die. Everyone who has followed Christ for any length of time knows the truth and impact of those words. The price of faith may be embarrassment, hardship, and in some circumstances, violent death, as it was for Bonhoeffer and the cloud of witnesses who were martyred for the church. The signers of the Declaration of Independence offered up their lives, their fortunes, and their sacred honor for the founding of this country. We have to risk our lives, our fortunes, our honor, and our reputations to follow Christ. A disciple becomes *fearless*, aware that the future may contain suffering but unafraid because Jesus himself will walk just ahead of us. Jesus warned, "Whoever does not carry the cross and follow me cannot be my disciple."

Obedience to a Larger Will

Following Jesus means not only belief and trust, but also obedience. You follow Christ more nearly when you honestly say to God, "What you ask of me, I will give. What you call me to do, I will do. Where you want me to go, I will go." That doesn't mean being uptight. Pharisees pretended to themselves that they were obedient, but they were really only interested in letters and loopholes so they could achieve their own ends. Real obedience moves a person to pray every day to make God's will his or her own.

Jesus said, "Those who abide in me and I in them bear much fruit," and he referred often to the pruning and training that his "branches" had to experience. Anyone who has grown grapes, especially wine grapes, knows what Jesus was talking about. Grapes appear only on new growth, so every year after harvest, the vine-dresser has to cut off all the shoots and branches and burn them to avoid disease. The next year's branches and future grapes "abide" in the leafless T-shaped trunk all winter, waiting for the sun and rain to call them forth. Grapevine shoots that wildly take off on their own are called "suckers" because they pull nutrients away from the main stem and the fruitful branches, so they're whacked off by a good vineyard keeper.

Well, God is the one who keeps our vineyard, and not only does God prune back the shoots that take away our nourishment, he has already decided that we will grow and flourish. You and I were chosen. God knew you in your mother's womb—in fact, before the world was ever made, God knew what you would be and loved you. You're in the hands of the living God. Your life is hidden in that vine called Christ.

As wonderful as God's love is, however, that isn't the whole extent of being chosen. Being chosen also means being available to God, not just once a week for an hour, but every minute of your life.

When I was a little girl, we played a game called drop the handkerchief. We sat in a circle, and one child would skip around us, flapping us each with a handkerchief and saying, "I have a little dog, and he won't bite you, and he won't bite you, and he won't bite you . . ."

Eventually, she'd come to someone and say, "But he *will* bite you!" She would drop the handkerchief on that person, then run around the circle, trying to avoid having the new person tag her with the hanky. If she managed to sit down in the circle without being tagged, the new person had to be "it."

When God chooses you, you might feel as if you'd been tagged in that drop-the-handkerchief game. A God who won't bite you, and won't bite you, but *will* bite one of us. Once God drops the handkerchief on you, you are, as my grandson would say, dead meat. You don't just take up the handkerchief; you're also going to take up the cross. So maybe you're thinking "I'm glad God didn't choose me!"

Somebody—I feel certain that it was Mother Teresa—said that when you experience pain and trouble, that means God is kissing you. And here is the kiss: God said to his only begotten Son, "I will let you be despised and rejected in your own home town, and finally, I will watch you be crucified."

Who wants a God like that? In fact, how can I love a God like that?

But you can't yell "not it" retroactively. Now *you* have to take up the handkerchief and follow that will that is larger and more wonderful than your own.

Jeremiah fell into God's hands. He pleaded his youth, saying, "I'm only a child." Those whom God chose have always argued. Moses insisted that he was a terrible speaker and could never lead the Hebrew people. Isaiah claimed to be a man of unclean lips, living among a people of unclean lips. Saul said, "But am I not a Benjamite, from the smallest tribe of Israel?" Even Samuel cried out against being chosen: he said, "Whose ox have I taken? Or whose donkey have I taken? Or whom have I defrauded? Whom have I oppressed?"

God tagged Jeremiah to prophesy to people who weren't going to listen. God chose Paul to pull the Corinthian church out of its disorder, but since he had to write a second letter to that church, we know that they didn't listen, at least the first time. And finally, God chose Jesus to preach the mystery of the kingdom to people who not only wouldn't listen but tried to throw him over a cliff.

It's a terrible thing to fall into the hands of the living God. When God chooses, God says "I will burn your lips with hot coals. I will get you banished to another country, to live among strangers. I'll let you be beaten up and thrown into a cistern or sawn in half or thrown off a cliff or stoned to death."

Life would have been easier for the prophets and apostles without God. Jeremiah could have had a normal youth and grown up to be a happy man. Without God, Paul could have been a successful Pharisee, with high standing in the Sanhedrin and, since he was a Roman citizen, he might have become a good friend of the Herodian and Roman courts. And without God, Jesus would have been a happy Nazarene carpenter with a wife and sons to carry on his name.

Life would be easier for you without God. And though you are free to disobey God's decrees, you can't refuse to be chosen. Just as God put words in Jeremiah's mouth, God has chosen you and is putting words in your mouth. There's news, good news, for you to deliver to the world, the news that no matter what happens to us on earth, God goes with us to strengthen and sustain us and that when we get to our real lives, God will welcome us in. So even if God bites occasionally, God's love is better than anything the world can offer.

Growth in God

When God said, "I choose you," why did you respond? Why did I? Why did Jeremiah? Why did Jesus Christ respond to God's invitation to the cross?

Growth in God is sure death to the earthbound ego. Pruning can be painful, and being slashed back to the main stem feels like the end. But God is glorifying, not destroying us, making us more like Christ. "Abiding" in Christ as we wait for the springtime of heaven means that we live *his* life and constantly stretch toward God.

This ain't easy. We live in a culture of self-love and self-praise. Every magazine cover lists at least one article inside titled something like, "Ten ways to like yourself better." But a true disciple of Christ offers everything up to God and never believes he or she is the creative source of goodness. We may be able to take ten pounds off on our own, but only Christ can carry us to the throne of

God, and that's where we want to go. A true disciple seeks to further the kingdom of God and hopes most for a chance to live in heaven where God is always glorified. A true disciple understands sacrifice.

Sacrifice can be small: you've made yourself a peanut-butter sandwich, and your child comes in hungry, so you give her your food. Or it can be great: your spouse has Alzheimer's disease, and you take early retirement in order to care for him or her. Every sacrifice for another person—"for the least of these"—is done for Christ. Each time we offer money, service, or time to the needy, to the work of the church, or to the spread of Christ's kingdom, we're making ourselves fit for the kingdom of heaven.

There are those who think they can be Christians by themselves, who say they can find Christ on the golf course or while fishing, or in the company of their families. But we see Christ face to face only in the Eucharist, which we can't do at home alone. And, as Jewish theologian Martin Buber says, we hear God only in the dialogue with others. It's in the Christian community that we come to know God and to be disciples of the Lord Jesus Christ.

In the first chapter of Acts, Luke takes us to the upper room, where the faithful gathered "in one accord" to wait for the Holy Spirit; after that, they met together constantly to eat their love feasts, to hear the disciples' teaching, to pray, and to gather in fellowship. (I wonder how many of us would have time for that kind of life today?) The author of the letter to the Hebrews admonishes us not to neglect our assemblies and meetings. And the church invites us to participate not only in the Eucharist but in one another's Christian lives.

Discipleship has its privileges, too. The first is experiencing a close, personal relationship with Jesus. Nobody knew Jesus the way the twelve apostles did. They traveled the dusty roads with him, spent the evenings talking with him, constantly turned to him for counsel, even argued with him. They slept where he slept and ate what he ate. And the experience empowered them to change the world. Jesus offers us the right of intimate relationship so that he, himself, is our constant companion, adviser, brother, and friend.

Prayers of petition for ourselves and others are a mark of our faith in the promises of Jesus Christ. Unlike deep meditation and adoration, petitionary prayer—asking a favor of God—means that we believe God cares about us as individuals. When we're children, we might ask God for anything we like because we see God as a combination of our mothers and Santa Claus. Later on, Christians usually begin to refrain from so much asking because it seems presumptuous. But when our faith is made more alive by the Holy Spirit, we begin to pray again for favors, usually beginning with intercessions. Only a true disciple can be absolutely positive of getting Christ's ear, just as Mary felt perfectly at ease to go to her son at Cana, saying "They have no wine." This shows why we can ask favors of God in prayer and ask how to pray effectively.

Who changed on the Mount of Transfiguration? Did Jesus attain a new degree of personhood? More likely, the three disciples who witnessed the scene changed so they could actually behold the beauty of the Lord. True disciples learn to see past the world's values and see Jesus in glory—not only on the cross for our redemption, but enthroned and practicing a greater ministry. Little by little, Christ reveals himself, preparing us for that day when we see him face to face.

Tevye, played by Zero Mostel in the musical *Fiddler on the Roof*, was constantly asking God "Why?" He did so as part of a long Jewish tradition that goes back at least to Moses: "Then Moses turned again to the Lord and said, 'O Lord, why have you mistreated this people? Why did you ever send me?'" (Exodus 5:22). The daughters of

Zelophehad, Joseph's heir, asked, "Why should the name of our father be taken away from his clan because he had no son?" (Numbers 27:4) Joshua, faced with a fierce army, asked, "Ah, Lord God! Why have you brought this people across the Jordan at all, to hand us over to the Amorites so as to destroy us?" (Joshua 7:7). Job, accusing God of letting chaos break out, cried, "Why have you made me your target?" (Job 7:20). Thus it was in that tradition that Mary, an intimate disciple of her Son, asked, "Son, why have you treated me this way?" A disciple reveals just how intimate is his or her relationship with Jesus by challenging him when life gets hard.

Going where Jesus goes may at first feel difficult. He goes to all kinds of prisoners, not only those in jail, but also those trapped by addiction, abuse, poverty, and despair. He goes not only to cathedrals but also to junk heaps, deathbeds, and homeless camps. But he also frequents places of great beauty: gardens, forests, oceans, and sky. The disciple who loves in close relationship with Jesus Christ will go wherever he goes—and will do whatever he does.

In the first chapters of Mark, we see Jesus living in a house where people crowded onto the porches, climbed in the windows, and came through the roof!

Why? Because all are welcome in the Jesus house. His disciples are welcome not only in Christ's spiritual house, but in the church he established. We are welcome to join the angels, archangels, and all the company of heaven in praise. We are welcome to exchange the peace of the Lord. And we are welcome individually and corporately at his altar, to partake of his body and blood. By exercising these privileges, disciples discover their role in the church and gain the skills to put their natural talents to use.

Sometimes Jesus spoke to others—including his mother—in a way that startles us. Christ's assertion of authority may not always be polite or attractive. Likewise, in the world around us, we encounter people and situations that anger, hurt, or shock us. These are all opportunities to practice God's brand of grace: forgiving the insolent child and even ignoring the behavior, just as Mary did when Jesus balked at furnishing wine for the wedding. We can practice the kind of grace God shows, as in Psalm 103:12: "As far as the east is from the west, / so far he removes our transgressions from us." The disciples were given the power to forgive sins in John 20; this shows how we, as modern disciples, can also be instruments of God's grace in this confused and broken world.

When the people of Israel returned to their country, Nehemiah admonished them not to weep over their sins and thus ruin the Lord's day. He advised them to sing, dance, eat well, and send gifts, "for the joy of the Lord is your strength." Modern life is sometimes so difficult that the thought of joy never crosses our minds. In fact, for many people in the twenty-first century, life is composed solely of work and worry. But Jesus teaches us unconditional love, which leads to total joy. The ecstasy many saints experienced in Christ's presence is available to all disciples who are willing to cast aside the false desires of the world and turn in love to him.

I don't love God because I'm successful—in fact, most days, I don't feel all that successful as a writer. I don't love God because I'm scared not to or because God gave me what I prayed for.

I love God because God, in the personhood of Jesus Christ, is so amazing, so compelling, that I have no choice. You can talk all you want about free will, but we're drawn to God the same way iron filings are drawn to a magnet, the way rivers head for the sea.

I once heard a theologian speak on why the mood of the Old Testament is so different from that of the New. He laughed and said, "Was God converted?"

No. But *I* was, have been, am being converted, over and over. I was lucky enough to grow up in the home of believers, so I knew Jesus when I was young. Or did I? Every day I see him more clearly and love him more dearly. The beliefs that I held onto as a child, and edged away from as a teenager, and thirsted for in middle age have become the faith of aging. I can't say my faith is finished, but my spiritual life has been through every phase of maturation, over and over, like rings of a tree.

I have answered God's call to come and die many times, and I have died and been restored always, so that I feel a little like the guy in the film *Groundhog Day*. He was so supercilious and self-absorbed that he had to keep reliving the same day until he learned how to be a human being. Each day he was in Punxsutawney, Pennsylvania and he took a piano lesson. During that process of repeating that day, he went from rank beginner to accomplished jazz pianist; he learned how to be kind to people and to quit believing he was king of the world.

Those of us who are struggling toward God are not so different. God's version of *Groundhog Day* will fool you because it never looks the same, so you don't know you're still learning how to love God, over and over again. The hero in the movie finally got it right, and he woke up on February 3. I've been repeating God's Now, albeit in different places and at different ages, and I know that one of these mornings I'm going to wake up someplace Else, the Else where we all want to go when we die.

So I fell in love with God, not once but over and over again. The childhood love I held for God was a lot like the feeling I had for my father. That has changed from a more earthly love to something mental, and now my spirit is waiting with delighted expectancy to see God.

Grace is not cheap: it's free. But living as a disciple can be costly, because God wants everything. One cannot ask to be a disciple, and then hold something back or continue in a sin or live a selfish life. To accept the free gift of grace and the privileges of discipleship means that God will start rearranging our lives, changing us, transforming our small, crooked selves into creatures of glory who can dwell forever in heaven's courts. Day by day.

CHAPTER FOURTEEN

The Contribution

Now we have received not the spirit of the world,
but the Spirit that is from God, so that we may
understand the gifts bestowed on us by God.
1 Corinthians 2:12

Your power is in your faith. Keep it and
pass it on to other bloods.
Molefi Kete Asante, *Ninja: The Way*

Y OU HAVE SPENT YOUR LIFE ACCUMULATING
the gifts of God. Now you can return them by offering your knowledge and talent and skill to the rest of humanity. Your gifts are unique, partly because you are unique and because you add to your skills and talents the age factor. Now, you need to build snowmen.

I was sick every winter in early childhood; sometimes I lay in my bed and sobbed with the pain in my ears. Antibiotics did not show up until World War II started, so my childhood earaches were a nightmare. My mother heated cloth bags of salt, and I used them like heating pads against my ears. I took down with that dreaded disease, mastoiditis, and while my parents and doctor worried about meningitis, I finally suffered through a mastoidectomy in the hospital and stayed there for three weeks afterward. Finally a doctor took my tonsils out, and I never had another earache. I remember waking up full of ether, throwing up and unable to swallow. Later my father carried me from the hospital to the car and then into the house, and pretty soon it started to snow.

Snow had never fallen on our Arizona town, at least not in recorded history. Until that evening. At midnight I woke up with my father rubbing the top of my head. He rolled me up in quilts so that I looked like a toothpaste tube and carried me to the front porch. And then he built me a snowman in the bright moonlight because he was afraid the snow would melt and disappear before morning.

That snowman is still there, in the Arizona high desert. As I dragged myself onto an airplane to fly to my father's funeral, I suddenly remembered the snowman. By the time I landed in San Diego, I was able to celebrate my father's life. I hope someone will someday celebrate mine, will remember some small deed I performed, some act of kindness. Death has no dominion over my father because once he ran straight up a hill to bring me a blue thistle, because he used to wake me up in the morning by singing "My Heart's in the Highlands," because he taught me to use a slide rule when I was nine, and because he built a snowman for me in the Arizona moonlight. When I think of him, I always want to recite E. E. Cummings's poem about how his father "lived his soul," and so love was "whole and more than all." My father lived his soul and also brought mine to life.

Our Turn to Love

Few of us had such a parent. A younger friend of mine was downright angry when I told her the snowman story. "That sounds like a fairy princess or something," she said with a sniff. Her shoulders shook with annoyance because she's seventy-two years old and never had anyone who tried hard to infuse her with life. Hers has been an average life, one without much real joy. The world around us is in terrible pain: broken promises and unfulfilled dreams have left shattered people and churches. Nobody ever built my friend a snowman in the moonlight or brought her a thistle; in fact, I don't think anyone ever did much for the lonely child inside her. Until now. It is my turn to show someone some extraordinary love.

You've undoubtedly heard "love thy neighbor" all your life, and maybe you've discovered, as I have, that both "love" and "neighbor" take on different meanings when you are age ten or thirty or fifty. Those meanings become supercharged at sixty or seventy. Now "love thy neighbor" doesn't just mean being kind or charitable. Now, God gives me a chance to affirm the community, to be one in Christ with you, to walk the extra mile, even if I'm not having a good time.

Why do I need to become more outgoing as I age? Because this is my last chance to offer my wit and wisdom and help and encouragement to the rest of the world. I can no longer get by hoping that my books are a boon to humankind while I withhold my presence from most of it. God is calling us out to ministry, and it's now or never.

Evelyn Underhill once said, "If we do not at least try to manifest something of Creative Charity in our dealings with life, whether by action, thought, or prayer, and do it at our own cost—if we roll up the talent of love in the nice white napkin of piety and put it safely out of the way, sorry that the world is so hungry and thirsty, so sick and so fettered, and leave it at that: even that little talent may be taken from us. We may discover at the crucial moment that we are spiritually bankrupt."

Our Ordinary, Necessary Gifts

What should you do when you do step outside your door? Well, you get wise as you age, so now you can stir that wisdom into all your other knowledge and skill and offer it to others. If you're a carpenter, you can not only advise people about building and framing and sawing; you can show them the tricks you've learned to make the work easier, and if they ask your advice, tell them what you know. Doctors can train young doctors not only in medical skill but in how to see their patients as whole people. Retired pastors can continue pastoral care with special attention to others their own age, encouraging them as they travel toward the end.

If you've been a homemaker all your life, you know stuff that other people need. You know how to pick up a baby without waking it, adjust erratic oven temperatures, grow African violets, scrape an apple to stop diarrhea, cure a cat of hairballs, iron a shirt, get wine stains out of carpets, or soothe an angry child—things you acquire only by practice or from someone like you. And your wisdom about children, spouses, and what's important in the household could make a younger person as wise as you are—and possibly minus some of the pains and trials you endured for this wisdom.

But just knowing and telling and advising aren't enough, aren't all you can do to contribute to your world. You're about to hear that word you dread: *volunteer.* Become a mentor or a foster grandparent, work in the hospital gift shop or mailroom, volunteer at your local historical society or national monument, and find out what your church parish needs.

You may be surprised at the warmth of your reception. Several years ago, I was trying to set up a library in our church parish, and I called for volunteers. A few days later, as I was trying to sort a pile of donated books, one of our elderly parish members appeared, saying she'd like to help. She was eighty years old, had a master's in library science from an eastern university, and had been a college librarian for forty years! I could have kissed that woman's feet. She organized the books, got her great-grandchildren to help shelve them, and directed the making of cards and pockets. She ran that parish library for the next ten years; after that, she and her ailing husband went to live with a daughter in another state. By then, she'd trained enough parishioners that the library has run smoothly to this day.

Being a mentor to a middle-school or high-school kid, or to a whole class, offers not only something fun for you but a real educational possibility for the kids. I never thought of mentoring until we had a school shooting four blocks from my house. Wondering what I could do—besides leaving a bouquet stuck in the high school's fence—I offered to teach kids to write. Now, a number of young writers come to me for help and instruction.

While visiting a nursing home, a friend of mine noticed a beautiful grand piano in the parlor. When she asked about a music program, a nurse said that someone had donated the piano but nobody could play it well. My friend, who is about seventy-five, began playing the instrument every Wednesday afternoon; she performed classical music and old-time favorites. By the third week, the room was full of people who wanted to sing—and two couples who danced to her music. Not only did she continue to play, she found two other pianists who could substitute for her or play on other days, and now the nursing home is well known around town for its fine music program.

Another man in our parish had been the president of a big corporation. Soon after he retired, he had lunch with a lawyer friend who was defending someone pro bono. The corporate man realized he had never done anything for free in his life; so he started by volunteering to do the audit on our church's books. Soon he became parish treasurer and conducted the yearly audit on our diocesan treasury. Today, he is the financial officer for our diocese, and he has trained—pro bono—ten other men and women who are helping with stewardship, balancing books, and good treasury administration. And he says he's happier than when he was making millions.

I suspect you have no idea how important your memories can be to your community or even to people all over the country. I had collected genealogical data about my family for years before I finally bought an easy software genealogy program so I could record the data on every ancestor. I started with fewer than a hundred people in the record and got acquainted with online resources and the free family-history centers run by the Mormons. Today, I have more than six thousand names in my chart; but what's more important, I learned how to export my gedcom, which is a record of every person in my software. With fear and trembling, I uploaded my record to Rootsweb, a free online genealogy center.

Within a week, I met a new cousin. I now correspond with cousins all over this country and have met a second cousin who has for several years lived only about ten miles from me. One man is my thirteenth cousin three times removed, but we both happen to love the church and music and politics, which we wouldn't have known had I not donated my information to all other genealogists. Each time I export an updated gedcom—a short process once I learned how—I get e-mail from people who want to know more, or who think we're connected, or who want to thank me for filling in the blanks in their own family records. My hobby has actually turned into a service to others.

One thing genealogy studies do is make you realize how connected we are. Even if we can't find the connection, we do know (as cited in *Time* and *Scientific American*) that everyone outside Africa was descended from a woman who lived ninety thousand years ago. So we're related and we need one another. I need what you know, and you need my expertise. And since time is running out, it's time to contribute to the community of humans. If you'll say "Okay, I'll build snowmen," God will show you a million hands reaching out, asking for help, asking to be filled with celebration, asking for everything you think or do or own.

CHAPTER FIFTEEN

Overcoming Death

We know that Christ, being raised from the dead,
will never die again; death no longer has
dominion over him.

Romans 6:9

I STOOD WITH MY HANDS ON MY HIPS, YELLING at God.

"Death sucks," I shouted. I don't know if God snickered, but I was dead serious. If we need to be transmuted from one form to another, why can't it be through something we like, something we can look forward to, be excited about, even long for? I look forward to seeing my children, to opening packages, to discovering an ancestor I didn't know I had. I'm excited about a new book or a writing friend's book contract. I love a day with nothing to do. I long for Christmas with my family and for the Eucharist. But I don't long for death or even court the idea.

In fact, if you want the truth, I dread dying. Being dead will be fine because I will be with God, but the process of dying—from ancient, infirm age or of some awful disease that ravages body and mind—is not my idea of how we should get, as Jonathan Livingston Seagull was so fond of saying, from here to there—here being life on earth and there being life after death or the resurrection, whichever comes first.

Shaking Hands with Death

Now that I'm aging seriously, I have to either make peace with God and death or go not gently but kicking and screaming into that good night. I keep telling myself what God told Blessed Julian of Norwich: that all shall be well. But is it "well" when planes crash and hundreds die? Is it "well" when the Israeli bulldozers demolish Palestinian houses? Was it well when the five-year-old child down my street was diagnosed with a fatal neurological disorder?

Don't strain my good humor, God says. *I said all SHALL be well, not that all is fine. Evil happens.*

Oh cool, I snarl. Pie in the sky bye and bye when I die.

I think I hear God sigh, and then silence in heaven, and without my willing to do so, I whirl to look at the crucifix over my desk. I gaze on it and know, at least for a split second that, indeed, all shall probably be well. In fact, I know for sure that all shall be well. The problem is the route I must take to that wellness. To make peace with God means to at least shake hands with, and at most embrace, death.

We are spared from death sometimes, but only temporarily. I presume Lazarus, dead in his tomb and then resurrected, had eventually to die again. We constantly experience what Thomas Moore in his book *Care of the Soul* calls "insinuations of death."

"Care of the soul requires acceptance of all this dying," Moore says. "The temptation is to champion our familiar ideas about life right up to the end, but it may be necessary to give them up to enter into the movement of death." Entering into the movement of death doesn't mean denying God or grace or resurrection; it means looking the event straight in the eye and saying, "I'm coming." And "all of this dying," as Moore calls it, includes the thousands whose lives end every day, people about whom we never think: old men in Thailand and soldiers in Afghanistan and babies in South Carolina and people who've had strokes in New York.

But we aren't going to an end, but to a beginning. "And just as it is appointed for mortals to die once, and after that the judgment," says the epistle to the Hebrews, "so Christ, having been offered once to bear the sins of many, will appear a second time, not to deal with sin, but to save those who are eagerly waiting for him" (9:27–28).

So there is life, and after that, Life; the problem is the abyss between. I can't, as Jonathan Livingston Seagull could, simply will myself across the chasm; it is filled with angry armed guards and nerve gas, guarded by three-headed dogs and rolls of razor wire. So I demand to go plead my case before the throne of God; and having heard me out, God says, *I gave you life.*

"That's the whole problem," I yell back. "You made me like life more than death. Life goes by too quickly."

A day or two ago, you were complaining that time was too slow.

But that was when I was bored or tired or at a workshop where I already knew the material. Time in general is too short, except for when it's too long, and on some days I think life sucks because death is waiting.

St. Paul said that the only meaning of his life was to testify to the good news of God's grace, and I wish I were that pure. But did Paul have a spouse and kids and grandkids? Did *he* have a great-granddaughter whose face is like a cameo and whose words are like the golden nails on which the Argonauts hung the golden fleeces? Did Paul have to figure out how to paint his living room with a torn rotator cuff?

No, because for him the grace of God was bigger and more beautiful than anyone or anything on earth. Well, then, does God expect me to be St. Paul?

No, God hollers down. *I expect you to be St. Kristen. Start disseminating grace.*

Being Christ for Others

Which means that I must become the best I can be—the most honest, the least selfish, the completely joyful woman I know how to be. I need to be more outgoing, less introverted, more forgiving, more encouraging. I need to quit squabbling with my husband over the condition of his bathroom and whether his jacket is still lying on the couch where he tossed it three days ago. I need to suffer fools more gladly and complain less.

So instead of concentrating now on just my own aging and inner life, instead of dwelling for twenty-four hours every day on my impending death, I have to perform mitzvoth for the suffering. I have to make life less a game of solitaire and more one where I'm on the mountain, feeding multitudes, not only with loaves and fishes but with joy. I am part of a royal priesthood, offering myself up to Christ for love of the world.

That's how I get across the abyss between life and death: not standing in front of a calendar or watching the clock, mourning the passing of my own life, but by being what I can be to someone else.

Can I do it? Can I fill others with such exquisite memories that at my funeral, they will stand up and say their lives were better because of mine? I can't do it in my small children because now I have no small children. But grandchildren are out there, and young writers and even old writers who need my help. God doesn't want me for a servant, because I am God's daughter; but the people around me need servants. Can I do it, now that I'm old and in some stage of decrepitude?

Not alone, I can't. But give God an inch and God takes a mile. Yes, death is inevitable, and that fact shapes my spiritual life. Yes, death is awful, and the idea of passing through it is terrifying. The abyss is dangerous and the process unpleasant or maybe even terrifying. But death will have no dominion because I will have chosen life, and giving life, not once but again and again and again, daily and yearly, until the moment when I stand before the throne, grinning like a fool and celebrating my salvation.

PART IV

To See Thee Face to Face

❧

Thus the LORD used to speak to Moses face to face, as one speaks to a friend.

Exodus 33:11

CHAPTER SIXTEEN

Letting Go

Now the Lord is the Spirit, and where the Spirit of
the Lord is, there is freedom.
2 Corinthians 3:17

The freedom now desired by many is not freedom to
do and dare but freedom from care and worry.
James Truslow Adams

ZECHARIAH THE PROPHET WAS AMONG THE people who returned to Jerusalem from captivity in Babylon and Persia. He urged them on to rebuild their temple so they could again participate in worship of Yahweh and prepare for the coming of the messiah. The people had gone from one kind of captivity to another. They were back in their homeland, but the city walls were rubble, the nation was constantly involved in small wars and border skirmishes with their close neighbors, the farms and vineyards stood desolate, and worst of all, God was apparently gone from Jerusalem.

The people were imprisoned by memory and narrowness and inertia.

These people were hopeless and despairing, but Zechariah said, "Rejoice greatly, O daughter Zion! Shout aloud, O daughter Jerusalem! Lo, your king comes to you; triumphant and victorious is he, humble and riding on a donkey, on a colt, the foal of a donkey." The Messiah, the Christ, was coming! And once again God would make their temple his dwelling place. Zechariah said again, "Return to your stronghold, O prisoners of hope; today I declare that I will restore to you double" (Zechariah 9:12). Prisoners of hope? Is that an oxymoron? Yes, because hope was all they had in their captivity. The prophets had preached hope, but though they read and recited hopeful passages, they felt unable to move themselves toward freedom, at least the kind of freedom that gives you the strength to go on. Hope held them in place but also made them afraid to move. So God sent them a message: "As for you also, because of the blood of my covenant with you, I will set your prisoners free from the waterless pit" (Zechariah 9:11). God was on the move, waiting to engulf with love the people of Judah. Just as God is waiting now to engulf the people of America.

And riding on a donkey. God was going to come, not in a fiery chariot or on wings of gold or with myriads and myriads of angels. "Lo, your king comes to you," the prophet said, "triumphant and victorious is he, humble and riding on a donkey." Well, now, they wondered, how can God be triumphant and humble at the same time? And what is this donkey business?

A donkey is shaggy and nondescript, hardly the vehicle for a victorious king, but the sight of Jesus riding into Jerusalem on "a donkey, a colt, the foal of a donkey," which means the animal wasn't even a powerful half-horse mule. And if we want to imitate Christ, we're supposed to ride on donkeys instead of beautiful horses or maybe even SUVs. In other words, even when we share Christ's triumphs and victories, we need to maintain our humility.

In fact, I knew a man who called himself a donkey. The late Reverend David du Plessis came to be known as "Mr. Pentecost" when first he walked into the National Council of Churches meeting and offered to talk to the mainline clergy about God's spiritual gifts and then later spent five years at the Vatican, advising Pope Paul VI and his cardinals about the charismatic movement. Du Plessis said that when he was a boy of fourteen in his home in South Africa, missionaries came to his parents' church, asking for donkeys. They needed to take supplies on the mission journeys over the mountains, where they were spreading the Good News of Jesus Christ, and they asked churches for either donkeys or the money to buy donkeys, because they were very poor. David's parents didn't have enough money to help, so they gave their son as a donkey to carry food and Bibles over the mountains to the unchurched. David became the beast of burden. And he got the nickname David the Donkey, a name everyone used for him whether they knew the history or not.

Shortly before David's death, he and I taught at the same conference. I reminded him that I'd heard him tell the donkey story; and he said, "Well, this old donkey is still carrying Jesus around." In old age, David knew no lighter burden than Jesus Christ. And he was as humble and nondescript as a shaggy little beast of burden.

To carry Christ around gave David freedom from human despair and want and made him ready for heaven. He also knew that to carry Jesus around you have to put down any other possession or person or burden you're carrying. To get ready for the kingdom of heaven, you have to detach, let go of what has always mattered to you on earth.

Easing Our Grasp

Detachment sounds easy yet is nearly impossible to accomplish. You have to care and let go at the same time, and that double process is accompanied by pain. If you have children, you said goodbye to them when they left home; acquiescing to your own exit from their lives is a lot harder. When I look at my kids and grandkids at a holiday dinner, the pain I feel about leaving them is palpable. My great-granddaughter is three, and I would love to see her grow up.

But I have to let go of this life in order to enter the next. Some people face the end with gladness that heaven is close, and others have to be dragged protesting into eternal life because they can't detach from the world. We all have to start now, especially in these later years, releasing people and things and money and even ideas, because hanging onto the past can prevent our entering the future.

I remember the climactic scene in the film *The Secret of Roan Inish*. A little wild boy, sought by his family for several years, appears on the beach. He's nudged forward by the magical seals he has lived with; he looks back at the wild, cold sea, looks up at the storm pouring out of the heavens, and looks at his family, whom he has never known. Finally he runs into his grandmother's open arms. They wrap him in warm blankets, and his big sister holds him, feeds him a nourishing soup, sings to him, and enables him to say his first word: her name. He had to let go of one life in order to become what God made him to be. And we'll never be free, fit for heaven, until we leave the sea and go willingly into God's arms. So we have to find strategies for detaching.

From the beginning, humans have insisted on freedom. And God allows that. We have the gift of free will, and we're dead set on using it. But God is out to capture us. Oh, we're running free, all right. We have the freedom to be imprisoned by depression and despair, the freedom to sin and die, the freedom to live in utter hardship. God wants to bring us home, feed and nurture us, and restore us to the heavenly family.

Letting go of this life is one more journey, a spiritual trek that takes you from this country to the far one. Your love of life and the people in it strives with your love for

God, taking you two steps forward and one step back. Somewhere around the age of seventy you may realize that the die is cast and that you must set your face toward eternity in the same way Jesus set his face toward Jerusalem. As the old song about following Jesus says, "No turning back, no turning back."

It's not a journey of just one step. You don't have to give up life today, then lie down and die. You just have to start easing your grasp. Because letting go of life doesn't mean becoming limp and uncaring and depressed. Letting go isn't the same as giving up, isn't a weak "OK" to God. To let go of life means that you trust God for the rest of your time.

I suspect that the first step in letting go is beginning to get rid of your stuff. You look around the house and shudder: every surface is covered with what that decorator on TV calls house dandruff: chachkas and knicknacks that creep out of shelves and begin to occupy tables and walls and every available inch of space. By the time you're sixty or seventy, you probably have too many dishes. And chairs. And books, which are often the last things you can part with.

You may even move from a big house to an apartment or retirement village or just a smaller house. That means you have to give your kids whatever they want from the old home place, or dump it in a storage unit, or have a garage sale and ship the culls to a charity. Hand your daughter the silver salad tongs. Give your granddaughter the encyclopedia. Offer your young neighbor your collection of salt shakers. Phew. All that junk, gone at last! You've taken your first step in the journey.

Relinquishing Control

And then you let go of control. You not only refuse the presidency of your book club, you quit persuading people to do anything. You stop giving advice. When your neighbor asks if buying a house is a good idea, you find out what he really wants to do instead of telling him it's a seller's market and he should keep saving. If you're a real manipulator and have always been a heavy controller, withdrawing your iron hand may prove painful or even make you physically ill. But oh, what a relief it is when you realize that you no longer have to manage the universe. The solar system will continue to function without your attention, and your grown kids will love having the freedom to make their own decisions without your interference.

Dorothy L. Sayers once noted that people who make other people their job are dangerous, and I've said since I was a teenager that the most dangerous person in the world is someone who knows what's best for me. So if you're still managing and manipulating and bossing other people, it's time to stop. You won't be here to control them after you die, so you'd better let them practice their freedom now so they'll know how to act on their own.

Control has its extremes. I know a seventy-year-old divorced, childless woman who lives with her mother, who is ninety-two. The mother still runs her daughter's life, and the daughter, who is elderly, still acts like a compliant child, even letting her mother choose her clothes. And the mother brags about having "run off" her daughter's allegedly worthless husband.

You may be one of those rare people who never tries to make other people do what you want them to, if you want them to do anything. But most of us have some guile in this department. Maybe you "surprise" your granddaughter with a girlish dress—because deep down, you don't think a little girl, especially your granddaughter, should go to school (and certainly not to church) in jeans that bag at the ankle.

Recently I hosted a party to honor someone, and I invited all our oldest mutual friends. One of the friends took it upon herself to invite yet another woman, one whose company I had never particularly enjoyed and who had hurt me terribly; a gushy, shallow, backbiting woman I didn't wish to have at the party. When I spoke to my friend of my shock at her issuing an invitation without asking me, she said, "But we'll all enjoy her and it will be good for many reasons." She had decided what was best for me: she wanted me to open my arms to the woman, which was a controlling and manipulative decision. I managed to get through the party, but I was annoyed—not at the gushy woman but at my friend for maneuvering and managing a life that wasn't hers. I hope that when she gets older she'll start letting go of control, or she'll be unprepared to let go of her life.

Maybe your control doesn't extend to others but you're a hard taskmaster with yourself. That invisible judge you carry on your shoulder criticizes everything you do and tells you daily that you don't measure up. Now, as you let go and detach yourself from life, dump the judge. So you're not perfect? So what? You have nothing to lose by spending your later years as yourself. The next time that unpleasant little voice suggests that you did it wrong or said it wrong, try the shrug. Shrug and say aloud, "Oh, well." Do that enough times and you may actually enjoy your old age.

Leaning toward God

After you relinquish control of people and things both inside and outside you, you must continue to serve and give, but you begin to tilt a little. Instead of being torn equally by God and your life, you lean ever so slightly toward God. You've always known that you were surrounded by angels; now you can almost see and hear them. The spiritual world around you is more real, and you hear the company of heaven calling your name, urging you forward. You start listening to the tender voice of Jesus Christ, whose arms are open wide to receive your death. The world is beautiful, but it is also a prison in which your immortal soul is confined and curbed. As much fun as life can be, you're really in captivity, waiting for the hangman.

My mother never let go of control and never accepted anyone's death. After my father died, she removed his picture from her sight. When she was in the nursing home, I took some framed snapshots of the two of them to her room. She kept them turned down on the table, saying she felt too sad when she looked at his face, because he was gone (at that point, he had been dead twenty years). She couldn't talk about him; his life had been for nothing, apparently, because it had ended. Mother saw death as a flaw in my father's and in her parents' lives. But death is a portal, not a flaw. A door through which we'll enter our real lives.

Letting go and accepting that life has an end doesn't make you passive. Now you can live out your time with as much passion as possible, doing whatever makes you and the people around you happy. You can give gifts with no strings attached, have friends you needn't control, and face every day with courage because you know that Someone is actually doing the work for you.

CHAPTER SEVENTEEN

Longing

My soul longs, indeed it faints
for the courts of the LORD;
my heart and my flesh sing for joy
to the living God.

Psalm 84:2

If I am a son of God, nothing but God will satisfy
my soul; no amount of comfort, no amount of ease,
no amount of pleasure will give me peace or rest. If
I had the full cup of all the world's joys held up to
me and could drain it to the dregs, I should still
remain thirsty if I had not God.

G. A. Studdert Kennedy, *The Wicket Gate*

ONE OF THE MAJOR DIFFERENCES BETWEEN Christianity and the Asian religions of Buddhism and Hinduism is the Christian respect for longing. While a brilliant, devout Buddhist such as the Dalai Lama has

taught himself to defeat desire, I am impelled by wanting; and my wanting leads me to Christ.

Longing That's Holy

Blaise Pascal, the seventeenth-century physicist and
mathematician, felt longing when he was a young man.
He wrote, "Within each one of us there is a God-shaped
vacuum that only God can fill."

K. C. Cole knew that longing also, and in her book
The Hole in the Universe, she writes, "There is a hole in
the universe. It is not like a hole in a wall where a mouse
slips through, solid and crisp and leading from somewhere to someplace. It is rather like a hole in the heart,
an amorphous and edgeless void. It is a heartfelt absence,
a blank space where something is missing, a large and
obvious blind spot in our understanding of the universe."

Finally, the theologian Huston Smith, building on
Pascal's ideas, says in *Why Religion Matters*, "Searching
for an image of the divine that will fit, [seekers] paw over
various options as if they were pieces of a jigsaw puzzle,
matching them successively to the gaping hole at the

puzzle's center. . . . They keep doing this until the right 'piece' is found. When it slips into place, life's jigsaw puzzle is solved."

What each of these writers was talking about is the kind of longing for God that begins as a sense that something's missing; the feeling expands and can even take over a life, as it did Pascal's. Because of their yearning, their wistfulness for God, human beings have tried everything from monasteries to orgies. Surely, we think, surely I'll find it if I keep looking. And on this side of the barrier between life on earth and life beyond, we discover that the puzzle piece will not completely slip into place.

Unlike our Buddhist and Hindu counterparts, we think that longing is a good thing. Rather than trying to discard all desire, we try to erase compulsive worldly attachments and yet heat up our aching for God. While a Buddhist might say that such a longing for God shows a karmic failure, the Jew or Christian who hungers and thirsts for the Lord celebrates that longing. The Psalmist said, "Whom have I in heaven but you? / And there is nothing on earth that I desire other than you" (Psalm 73:25). And A. W. Tozer, an evangelical Protestant preacher who drank at the wells of the great mystics, prayed in his book *The Pursuit of God:*

O God, I have tasted thy goodness, and it
has both satisfied me and made me thirsty
for more. I am painfully conscious of my
need of further grace. I am ashamed of my
lack of desire. O God, the Triune God, I
want to want Thee; I long to be filled
with longing; I thirst to be made more
thirsty still.

Tozer was ashamed, not of his desire, but of his failure to want, to long, to thirst. And his prayer still works for me.

They say that Christ spoke to Aquinas from the cross in the cathedral at Mainz; onlookers swore they heard Christ ask the praying Aquinas, "What would you have?" And Aquinas answered, "Thee only. To see thee face to face." After that he called his work in the *Summa Theologica* "straw." His hymns, such as "Humbly I Adore Thee," are full of his longing, with words that call Christ the "verity unseen" whose glory is hidden in the shadows. Aquinas confesses his faith in the salvific work of the atonement by saying, over and over, in every hymn and poem, *Someday*. Someday, he will see not a reflection of God or an image of God; someday, he will see God face to face. Meanwhile, he has to keep the prize before him by faith in the biblical promise:

> *Taste and touch and vision to discern thee*
> *fail; faith that comes by hearing pierces*
> *through the veil. I believe whate'er the Son*
> *of God has told: What the Truth hath*
> *spoken, that for truth I hold.*

I'm with Aquinas. What I want is seraphim darting around with their tongs full of hot coals and elders throwing down their crowns. I want to hear the call of "Holy, holy" and the choirs singing, "Blessed is the Lamb who was slain." Most of all, I want God—in person and on the throne. I want to see God, to see God face to face. When I get to heaven, I'm not going to look for my relatives or friends who went before me. I'm going to kneel down and look at God. No wonder my guardian angel keeps her face turned continually toward God and sees me only as a reflection in God's eyes; seeing God satisfies every longing, even that of angels. Once I see God, I'll never be hungry or thirsty or bored again, never wish or want again, never reach for something undefined again. I will have it all.

Pain in the Meantime

But until then, I have to live with the longing and ask God to be the anesthetic for its pain. And the older I get, the more defined the God-shaped vacuum will become. When I was a child, the empty place wasn't so clear; perhaps, like the bones in my skull, the sutures around the empty place hadn't closed yet. And when I was a young girl, the answer lay in the mystery and joy and pain of love. As I ripened into full adulthood, I began to fill myself by writing. But I always knew I wanted something else.

We identify the longing as kids, when we look at the first star and whisper "Starlight, star bright, first star I see tonight, I wish I may, I wish I might have the wish I wish tonight" and then we add our list of wishes: a rabbit, a horse, a bicycle, a Game Boy, a room of our own. We make wishes and then take deep breaths to blow out our birthday candles. But a rabbit or a horse or a Game Boy, even if it appeared on the spot, wouldn't render us wishless for the rest of our lives. We'd just keep thinking up new wishes, until the day we say, "I don't really want anything. Just God."

Thee only. To see thee face to face.

The psalmist's "hart that longeth for the waterbrook" has nothing on me. I've spent my whole life trying, as all but a few rare souls do, to fill that universal hole with something: college, love, marriage, sex, church, friends, art, music, writing, food, teaching, photography, crossword puzzles, computers, reading, wildflower identification, and travel—to name only a few of the hoped-for vacuum fillers. And nothing was ever enough. Money isn't enough and neither are sex or recognition or adulation. That ache inside, that vibrating emptiness somewhere behind the sternum, can be filled only with God.

And it never is, while we're on earth. There's the tension we have to live in, trying to create meaning between the emptiness and the filling, which we require death to achieve. Until I am before the throne of God, that hunger will never be alleviated.

Yes, I can take the edge off the pain of longing by getting as much of God on earth as possible. I can study the Bible and experience God through Scripture. I can pray and feel the Presence all around and through me. I can look for and listen to God in the dialogue with other people. And not only can I do these things, I must.

The God of Right Now

If I had a hologram of God and dropped it and broke it, each shard of the hologram would contain all of God. So although God is waiting for me on the other side of my death, God is also hidden in plain sight, and I can at least be half full here, now. Maybe I can't have all of God all at once, but I can at least have my shard.

Each of us has a puzzle to work out, as Huston Smith said. We can take the major pieces of our lives and see where God is dancing in the midst of them. Here are the pieces of my particular puzzle: a semi-homeless woman who holes up where I turn to go to church on Sunday mornings; a labyrinth in our churchyard near where my mother's ashes are scattered; a stack of unanswered mail; an asthma inhaler. All these are elements in my week, all entrances to the kingdom of heaven, all places in which to look for Christ himself. Now what I have to do is find out how I get more of God by dealing with these things.

I wish it were easier. Like physicists, I want a Theory of Everything, a theory that will lead me to the throne of God before I die. I want a pattern I can lay over my life, so I can see how one thing affects and depends on another, throughout the galaxy or beyond. They tell us that if a butterfly moves its wings a millionth of a centimeter, the entire universe is changed. So when I walk that labyrinth in the churchyard, by movements and my breathing I change not only my own spirit but the solar system—and even the galaxy—as well. I use air that then has to be recycled by the exchange process because there's a finite amount of air on the earth. While I walk the labyrinth, I may breathe the same air that Jesus or Hitler or Marie Antoinette once breathed.

If that butterfly moved its wings a hair and made an impact on the universe, then something must happen when I pray or sing or dance. C. S. Lewis once wrote that every decision we make moves us toward or away from God. Every movement I make should be taking me closer to the God I long for. Each step should carry me forward to the point that, one day, when I have learned to love God more than life in this poor old body, God will say, "Come," and I will go.

If I am not seeking God through every part of my life—the homeless woman, the labyrinth, even my physical limitations—then my longing for God can become mere attitude: grouchiness, general displeasure, and annoyance because nothing I see and nobody I know is what I want them to be. Instead of looking for God, I might turn that discomfiture into a critical spirit that picks on other people.

A wounded stag will race into the wood, and a true hunter will track the trail of blood and hoof prints until he finds the deer. God the Son is wounded, in fact, he has five clear wounds acquired on the cross; he is rushing ahead, preparing a place for us but also bleeding, bleeding. We'd better get tracking—not to give a six-point stag the coup de grâce, but to worship at his feet, to see him face to face.

CHAPTER EIGHTEEN

The Bread of Life

And King Melchizedek of Salem brought out bread
and wine; he was priest of God Most High.

Genesis 14:18

He is The Bread sown in the virgin, leavened in the
Flesh, molded in His Passion, baked in the furnace
of the Sepulchre, placed in the Churches, and set
upon the Altars, which daily supplies Heavenly
Food to the faithful.

St. Peter Chrysologus

ONE CHRISTMAS WE HAD SUCH A HARD freeze that cars slid across roads, kids fell down when they played outside, and some churches even canceled their midnight Mass. Most of our winters don't bring snow or hard frosts. But the day after Christmas, when the sidewalks were coated with slick ice and the lawn had turned into a field of sharp little spikes, we watched birds trying to scratch for food. They couldn't even turn over the maple leaves that were frozen to the ground. Several dead robins already lay in the yard, and one little chickadee gave up. He just puffed up his feathers, closed his eyes, and apparently waited for death. I tried to walk to a store, two blocks away, for birdseed, but I fell twice and went back to the house, imagining a spring without birds to sing and eat up the harmful insects and build houses under the eaves of my garage.

"We've got to feed those birds," we said, and we hauled out the leftover Christmas breads. We chopped up an uncut stollen and a braided Finnish rye and laid the fragments on the railing of my daughter's deck. The chickadees fluttered to eat, even the little one that looked half dead. They ate, squawked at one another, and quarreled over territory, but these weren't greedy creatures; they were starving. A robin came but kept its distance as it gulped down some crumbs, then flew away with a morsel in its beak. The big starlings came, their beaks open as they panted, their eyes glazed. They were so weak their yellow legs had trouble perching on the railing, but soon they'd eaten everything. We opened the freezer and chopped the last of the Christmas *bûche*, a package of tortillas, and some cookies. We mashed and chopped every starchy thing we could find in the larder, and all day creatures of the air came and ate their fill. They chirped and squawked and fluttered, and when we went to bed, we knew that those birds would live at least overnight.

The freeze broke the next day, Sunday; warm air from somewhere like Montana or Wyoming heated as it moved down the barometric slope and began to melt the ice. The streets were wet but no longer slippery, so we got in my car and headed to church. We were a few minutes late and crept behind the procession into a cloud of incense and song. At the rear of the church, on a credence table, stood a cruet of wine and a ciborium full of Communion wafers, and I knew then that I, too, was starving, that I too was desperate and would have to close my eyes and wait for death if I didn't soon have the Bread laid on my tongue.

Like Hungry Birds

That craving has to be more urgent in old age. We're not fooling around here with what the Eucharist is for. We have to have it to keep us alive and to make us alive in the next world. The Eucharist means "Thanksgiving," but it also means life in Christ, especially for those of us whose memories go back sixty years. We want not only to stay alive but to be alive as long as we live, alive in mind and body and spirit. The elements of Communion are the staff of our lives.

Catherine of Siena said, "You have left Yourself wholly to us, as food, so that we will not fall through weariness during our pilgrimage in this life, but will be fortified by You, celestial nourishment." That celestial nourishment has carried me through my life, from my first Communion onward, and will, I hope, be the last thing I know on earth: the Host slipped between my lips as I lie on my deathbed. Food for the journey. And in the meantime, my life is enhanced by the paschal repetition.

Old people are like that flock of hungry birds that needed food, and God left himself as our feast, turned himself into crumbs for our celebration. We flock around and, like birds, argue over territory and theology and method. We fight among ourselves in the church about whether we should receive both kinds and whether we should take the Bread in our hands or on the tongue. We chirp and squawk and flutter dangerously at one another over how the elements are transformed and what the date of Easter should be. We quarrel over how old a child should be to receive Communion and whether that child should understand the mystical components of the events.

But despite our beaks and claws and loud shrieks, the Eucharist remains, in the words of the Vatican II report, "the summit and source of the Christian life." The simple acts of thrusting your hands out for a thin wafer of unleavened bread and grasping the chalice for a sip of wine are what keep you alive. Old age is strengthened and bettered by the simple elements of bread and the juice of the vine. And you are the one who has to complete the Eucharist. You are compelled by grace to get out of the pew and walk to the altar rail, and if you are in a wheelchair or can't walk to the altar, you have to ask for the elements to be brought to you. You take Communion. Body and Blood stand waiting in the sanctuary and will not come to you unless you go toward them, at least in spirit.

Like the Prodigal Child

In this action, you become the prodigal. Indeed, you may have squandered the inheritance God gave you, not in riotous living like the son in Luke's story, but in other ways. I don't know how you fritter away and trivialize your life, but I can while away much of an hour on my computer, playing solitaire, or staring at CNN. If I walk up into the woods because I'm mad at my husband or agent or publisher, or I'm having a bad writing day, I might fail to notice the lacy ferns and the towering dark green Douglas firs or the alders that quake with bird life. I can mooch around the house in my pink sweats, popping potato chips and wishing I had more money, and ignore the heartfelt letters from readers that are piled on my desk.

And having squandered my divine inheritance, my daughterhood, I suddenly notice poverty. *I'm starving,* I say. I lament my situation and, after a time of self-absorption and narcissistic pity, start home. I plod along, practicing the words I'm going to say to God, muttering "Our father who art . . ." But when I finally get to the altar rail, I see God running—*running* toward me. The ministers stand with the silver patens and chalices in their hands, and as soon as my mouth is full, God runs to greet me, clothes me in satin, puts his own signet on my finger, and says, "She was dead, but now she is alive!" The Father has paced up and down in the road for months, years maybe, and is willing to run toward me as soon as I appear over the horizon. He is willing to offer more than I ever hoped for, but I have to make Eucharist by appearing in the road, or aisle, and stumbling toward home.

We are all prodigals because we are sinful, unhealed, lacking wholeness. But the substantial and astonishing grace of Eucharist heals and makes us whole, washes our sins in blood, and then turns our record white as snow. The bread and wine transform us daily from mean-spirited little birds into immortal beings who, on the last day, will be raised up incorruptible.

And the greatest miracle of all is that I am kept alive and made immortal through something I don't really understand. Like the chickadees and kinglets and robins, like the big, unsteady starlings that staggered onto the rail of my deck, I don't really understand where my food comes from. Oh, I know we buy our wafers from a Carmelite monastery here in town and the wine from a local vineyard; but I am unaware of just how they become the Body and Blood of Christ. And I don't have to know, don't necessarily even want to. I can sidestep Aristotle's laws of transubstantiation or Plato's absolute universals. I would rather eschew arguments about whether the change is physical or spiritual.

We could fight forever about whether Jesus' meaning in "This is my body" and "This is my blood of the new testament" was literal or figurative, physical or spiritual. I'm not a theologian, and I can tell you anyhow I'd rather see than be one. I don't want a theory or a systematic theology that purports to tell me the steps by which what was bread a second ago suddenly contains God's own DNA. I'm not saying that I prefer ignorance to knowledge or bewilderment to understanding. I grasp the principle, but I don't really want a wordy explanation because all I know is that what happens, happens.

How do I know it happens? Because my spiritual life is alive, fed by something outside myself. I am a starving bird, and a miraculous hand just put out bread and meat for me. I am doomed and know that I'm doomed until Sunday morning when suddenly grace jumps down off the cross and offers himself to me in the form of food.

❧

Like the Original Story

Scoffers like to point out that almost every pre-Christian mystery religion had a resurrection and a love feast of bread and wine: Mithra, Dionysus, the Eleusinian Mysteries, Cybele, and Osiris. But C. S. Lewis, who brought down every argument against Christianity, said that these myths, and many pre-Christian pagan practices, were "good dreams" that God sent for centuries in order to create readiness for the real thing. Myth, or good dreaming, projects visions of wholeness restored through divine action. This was a kind of remembering forward, a sense of truth even before the Truth manifested itself. The spirit of good dreams can make us wish that something of this sort might be true and prepare us to discover that at one time, the story came true.

God did say, after all, "I am sending you grain, wine, and oil, and you will be satisfied; and I will no more make you a mockery among the nations," and "Grain shall make the young men flourish, and new wine the young women." God is a god of things, of matter. God didn't use moonbeams and fairy dust to nourish us, but the basics of bread and wine. God transformed them to become food for our aging bodies and souls. I will probably live another twenty years or more, but how I live will be influenced by Christ's interaction with me in Communion.

The original communion meal was probably a Passover seder, at which lamb, sacrificed by a priest, was eaten with unleavened bread and bitter herbs and wine. In Luke's Gospel, Jesus says, "I have eagerly desired to eat this Passover with you before I suffer; for I tell you, I will not eat it until it is fulfilled in the kingdom of God" (22:15).

The Passover dinner Jesus ate has been depicted by many painters, including Leonardo da Vinci, Pablo de

Céspedes, Salvador Dalí, and Emil Nolde. The de Céspedes is full of dark Spanish tragedy, the Dalí rendering has an eternal, dreamlike quality, the da Vinci is irreparably "restored," and the Nolde intense and almost lyrical. All depict the so-called Last Supper, which should probably be called the First Supper, since it was the original Eucharist, the first memorial of our redemption, the *panis angelicus,* bread from heaven.

I want that bread. I'm a mean little bird, I'm a prodigal daughter, I'm a starving blue heron and an exhausted writer. I want God to feed me, to pour life into my body again. I want it every Sunday. I think I'll take it any time I can get it; I'll join in the dance with its priestly movements, the altar girls and boys whisking back and forth or kneeling with their lighted torches, the crucifer boldly lifting the cross before the world, the fracture, the breaking, the breaking, the breaking of the Body of Christ, then the offering up, the hope, O God, yes, the hope, the hope . . .

And then God lies on my tongue, God's blood courses through my veins, and that supper becomes my instrument of grace, the source of my life. I will live another day, perhaps; but for sure, I'm going to live forever.

CHAPTER NINETEEN

Resurrection

Anyone who comes to me . . . I will raise them up
on the last day.
John 6:37–40

Stop worrying about the potholes in the road and
celebrate the journey.
Barbara Hoffman and Fitzhugh Mullan, *A Cancer*
Survivor's Almanac: Charting Your Journey

THE UNIVERSE AROUND US SINGS DEATH AND resurrection. Stars die and become black holes and give birth to new stars. Seeds fall into the earth and die, then spring up with changed bodies as alfalfa or African daisies or Jonathan apple trees. God's thumbprint is on all creation, telling the story of death followed by new and glorified life. God will honor and glorify those of us who honor and glorify God. Jesus stated early in his ministry, "This is indeed the will of my

Father, that all who see the Son and believe in him may have eternal life; and I will raise them up on the last day" (John 6:40). Jesus is already bringing about what his Father ordained long ago.

❧

The Universal Sense of Rebirth

Christianity is full of promise, inviting us to live in Christ forever. The author of a fourth-century document in what is known as the Nag Hammadi codices wrote, "What, then, is the resurrection? It is always the disclosure of those who have risen. For if you remember reading in the Gospel that Elijah appeared and Moses with him, do not think the resurrection is an illusion. It is no illusion, but it is truth! Indeed, it is more fitting to say the world is an illusion, rather than the resurrection which has come into being through our Lord the Savior, Jesus Christ."

Non-Christians also have a tradition of rebirth. The main contention between the Pharisees and Sadducees was that Pharisees believed in resurrection. When St. Paul was on trial, he called out in the council,

Brothers, I am a Pharisee, a son of
Pharisees. I am on trial concerning the hope
of the resurrection of the dead." When he
said this, a dissension began between the
Pharisees and the Sadducees, and the assem-
bly was divided. (The Sadducees say that
there is no resurrection, or angel, or spirit;
but the Pharisees acknowledge all three.)
Then a great clamor arose, and certain
scribes of the Pharisees' group stood up and
contended, "We find nothing wrong with
this man. What if a spirit or an angel has
spoken to him?" (Acts 23:6–9)

Islam especially embraces the story. The Qur'an says
that the day of resurrection will be the occasion when
God's attributes of justice and mercy will be in full man-
ifestation; God will shower His mercy on those who suffered for His sake in the worldly life and believed that an
eternal bliss was awaiting them. But those who abused
the bounties of God, caring nothing for the life to come,
will be in "the most miserable state" (Holy Qur'an 28:60).

And the not so New Age idea of reincarnation is
nothing more than a humanistic version of resurrection

borrowed from the eastern religions' doctrine of karma, in which every sin has universal repercussions and has to be repaid. Life after death, instead of being a gift, then becomes a burden. Fortunately for us, Jesus is the payment for sin, and our karma is destroyed.

Like society in St. Paul's day, we have Sadducees in America; in fact, we have them in the church. They are "secular religionists" who deny the physical resurrection of Christ, aren't convinced of his divinity, and won't talk about life after death.

The Need to Believe

Every day, new seeds of doubt can spring out of nowhere, trying to take root in our minds. We have to be vigilant, and when doubts about life after this one rise up, we can't just try to ignore them or brush them aside as though they were spiritual lies buzzing around our heads. We have to engage the matter of resurrection head-on. In old age, we can't afford to be nonbelievers in the Resurrection. Those who say that "this is all there is" invite bitterness and hardness to take up residence in their souls, and now that we are on the verge of meeting God face to face, resurrection had better become the centerpiece of our faith.

What proof do we have? Have we ever met anyone who came back from the dead? Maybe. Thousands of people's "near death" experiences have been published, beginning with the 150 stories compiled by Dr. Raymond Moody in *Life after Life*. Some of the later stories sound a little New Age-y, but they all contain one message: life is empowered by love, and there's a powerful world beyond this one. Is that only, as some psychologists would say, wishful thinking by the ignorant? If so, then some awfully well-educated men and women have been ignorant.

Jesus also reminded us that God has already given us evidence—through the ram in the thicket that redeemed Abraham, and through God's covenants—that those who love God will not suffer death of the spirit. He told the story of the poor man covered with sores who lay at the gate of the rich man, dying of hunger. Both men died; the rich man went to torment in Hades, while the hungry one lay in the bosom of Father Abraham. The rich man in hell begged Abraham to send someone from the dead to warn his five living brothers; but Abraham said, "If they do not listen to Moses and the prophets, neither will they be convinced even if someone rises from the dead." And we are much farther along the heavenly trail: We have not only Moses and the prophets; we also have Jesus to show us the way.

Perhaps you just can't accept the concept. As far back as the fourth century, St. Augustine said, "No doctrine of the Christian faith is so vehemently and so obstinately opposed as the doctrine of the resurrection of the flesh." That opposition didn't begin during that era; in Acts 17:18–32, we read that "some Epicurean and Stoic philosophers" argued with Paul, and that when they had heard of the resurrection of the dead, some indeed mocked, but others said: "We will hear thee again concerning this matter."

Or maybe you believe in the Resurrection but you worry that you are unsaved and won't be resurrected. No matter how many times you confess your sins and receive absolution, your heart doubts even God's word, and you think, "I am going to burn forever and will never see resurrection." That's the favorite lie of evil. Even Brother Lawrence, that saintly monk whose treatise *The Practice of the Presence of God* has made a dynamic impact on thousands of lives, thought at one time that he was too sinful to be saved. Finally he decided to simply lay his sins before Christ and be at peace in God's love. And on the day of the Resurrection, I suspect Brother Lawrence will be among the great company of the exalted.

Sometimes we get mixed up about resurrection. I was once part of a panel where one of the other speakers kept equating life after death with resurrection (and I wasn't sure he really believed in either one); I know that he confused the audience. We believe in life after we die, if only because of Paul's statement that to be absent from the body is to be present with the Lord. And there are places such as purgatory where we get cleaned up for heaven. But we also believe in the resurrection of the physical body. Whatever comes right after death, resurrection has to come later, at least in earth time; in God's mind, where everything happens at once, the Resurrection is now. The kingdom of this world, as the Hallelujah Chorus reminds us, *is become* the kingdom of our God, and of his Christ.

According to the fourth Lateran Council, all people "will rise again with their own bodies which they now bear about with them." In the language of the church creeds and professions of faith, this return to life is called resurrection of the body for two reasons. First of all, the soul can't be said to return to life because it is eternal and therefore already alive. Second, the idea that resurrection happens only to the soul and not the body has long been considered by Christian orthodoxy to be a heresy. Resurrection is spiritual but also physical.

When Jesus went to Bethany after Lazarus had been dead for several days, he told Martha, "Your brother will rise again." Martha may have sighed; she wasn't a scholar, and though she believed in eternal life, she missed her brother.

"I know," she said. "We'll meet in the Resurrection."

I imagine that Jesus leaned toward her, his eyes intense as he pointed at himself. "Martha, *I'm* the Resurrection," he said. "I'm the Resurrection and I'm life." He probably gave her a minute and then asked, "Do you believe that?"

And Martha spoke the words that ring through the centuries, something like "Yes, Lord, I believe that you are the Christ, the Son of God, who is perpetually coming into the world."

Yet even though she affirmed her faith in his divinity, Martha didn't completely understand. When Jesus ordered the stone to be rolled away, she cried, "Lord, there will be a stench!" They didn't embalm in those days, and they did not yet have blocks of ice.

Jesus said to her, "Did I not tell you that if you believed, you would see the glory of God?" Although her belief was frail, Jesus honored it and let her see the first resurrection of the New Covenant. Actually, it was a sort of proto-resurrection, because it wasn't brought about by the risen Christ, didn't come in glory with clouds of angels and the blast of trumpets. In the raising of Lazarus we glimpse two signs of the new order in heaven and earth: natural law being overcome by a greater law of love, and the promise of new life to believers. We celebrate that promise in Easter, when we stand in awe of Christ's rising from the dead and in wonder at the possibility of our own raising.

Martha wasn't the first biblical character who stammered out her faith. Even in the Old Testament, God let us peep at God's final act of love for humanity. The prophet Daniel said, affirming not only resurrection but also judgment, "Many of those that sleep in the dust of the earth, shall awake: some unto life everlasting, and others unto reproach, to see it always." David exulted in Psalm 16:10, "For you do not give me up to Sheol, / or let your faithful one see the Pit," and in Psalm 17:15, "As for me, I shall behold your face in righteousness; / when I awake I shall be satisfied, beholding your likeness." Ezekiel saw the dry bones coming together, saw them take on flesh and breath. Isaiah 26:19 proclaims, "Your dead shall live, their corpses shall rise. / O dwellers in the dust, awake and sing for joy! / For your dew is a radiant dew, / and the earth will give birth to those long dead."

This means that no matter where your soul has been after death, whether in heaven or purgatory or just asleep, and no matter if you were embalmed or entombed, cremated or lost at sea, God will reassemble the atoms of your body and spirit into such splendor that what you were in life on earth might be compared to a slug or a crab. We aren't spirits imprisoned in bodies, as Greek philosophers believed; death is not the escape of the soul from a corrupt and disgusting physical structure. Your body today holds the mysterious promise of a resurrected form. I doubt if I'll be wearing the coral shorts and burgundy T-shirt I have on today; and I have faith that a resurrected life is a painless one, free of arthritis or diverticulitis. People who are confined to beds and wheelchairs with multiple sclerosis and stroke and postpolio in this life will, I am sure, go walking and leaping and praising God, like the man healed by Peter and John.

Resurrection Now

In the face of all this promise, we also have an opportunity for resurrection now, if we are willing to have the personality crucified also. If we, like Brother Lawrence, can lay our sins before God and ask that they be covered by the blood of Jesus, if we truly repent and make amends, then we can have a spiritual resurrection today. If we trust God, we will experience the death of our worst, darkest side and the rising of the godly self within us.

God will raise you, me, us, them up on the last day. And on this day, every day. God reaches out with resurrection written on the divine hand, offering eternal life with every breath we take. And the Bible reminds us that our first human breath was the breath of God, and that the last breath we take is only preparation for real life.

I don't know whether "on the last day" means earth's final moment or the ending of my own life; but since the world winds up for me on the day of my death, I'll take whichever comes first. D. H. Lawrence once said that "every parting means a meeting elsewhere." So endings on earth mean meetings in the beyond, in what my great-great-aunt Blanche always referred to as "the great by-and-by." I cannot but hope that the parting from this life means a meeting with God; and I will gladly go there in bondage, as a slave or as dust so long as I can see God on the throne.

So ignore the nonbelievers and doubters and the little Sadducee that lurks within you. Oh, yeah, they'll be there tomorrow morning when you awaken and wonder for a moment if you're still alive; you'll also probably notice that your life is winding down, and that maybe that's all there is. But if there is no life after this, why has every society, including even the Neanderthal who buried their dead with flowers and implements for the next world, believed that death was a beginning and that this wasn't the end? Haven't humans intuited from the very beginning that there is much more than this present life and that it waits for us on the other side of death?

Maybe the Resurrection is another universe, as close as my skin, as far away as Andromeda or farther. Maybe the space-time continuum is a twist in time and space, a conversion of matter, another continuum that is inexorably linked to this one. Take a strip of paper that's a different color on each side, give it a twist and glue the ends together, and you'll have a Mobius strip, where neither side either begins or ends. The mystery of resurrection may be like that twisted Mobius creation, where somehow what is eternal becomes only another side of what is temporal. I remember a quote by Victoria Moran: "This isn't the end of the story. It's just a twist in the plot."

CHAPTER TWENTY

The Sacrament of Time

Humble yourselves therefore under the mighty hand of God, so that he may exalt you in due time.

1 Peter 5:6

With time and patience the mulberry leaf becomes a silk gown.

Chinese proverb

MY FRIEND SAID, "I'M GLAD IT'S OVER." I was folding my mother's clothes into a box. Glad what's over? My six-day vigil, sleeping on a futon next to my mother's bed? My mother's life?

Mother's time ran out several years before she died. She was brilliant, a college professor and a journalist. She was a hopeful woman, always expecting something good to come around the corner, until my father died; then her chaos took over and she became confused. Old physical injuries crippled her body, and her mind was present only in surges.

We had a lot of uncomfortable history between us. But I was her only child, and when she collapsed and went to the hospital, I flew to California to see what I could do. She was recovering from a seizure and a small stroke; she could talk and move, but she was having a hard time thinking. I could tell when I got into her bills and papers. Her financial affairs—she'd always been meticulous in record keeping and bill paying—were a mess. Papers were squirreled into every drawer and cubby. She'd been ripped off by home health-care workers. She was underweight and intermittently crazy.

I brought her to Oregon and installed her in a nursing home, where she was unhappy. She was troublesome and manipulative, and some days I wanted to forget her; but she was my mother, after all, and I loved her.

At seven-thirty on a morning not too long before her eighty-seventh birthday, I was standing in the shower when I heard my answering machine pick up a message. It was the nursing home: Mother had had a stroke and gone to the hospital. When I got there, the doctor said she also had pneumonia, and he urged me to "let her go."

Mother had gone downhill severely, the doctor said, and I knew he was right. When my daughter had visited in August, she kissed her grandmother, who said, "Who are you?"

"I'm Susan," my daughter said, and Mother looked bewildered. Susan and Mother had always been close.

"Your hair is wrong," Mother finally said.

"She's fading away," the doctor told me at the hospital. "If she were my mother . . ."

He was young and earnest. His mother was probably fifty! Meanwhile, *my* mother looked at me the same way my dog does, trusting, smiling crookedly, occasionally waking to say through stroke-twisted lips, "Wy wuv woo."

After twenty-four hours of squirming and pondering, I allowed the hospital to remove her intravenous fluids and to stop treatment for the pneumonia. Time would have to stop. Soon I would be an orphan.

Because Medicare doesn't pay for people to die untreated in hospitals, we moved Mother back to the nursing home. I fed her red Jell-O and sips of water; I put lip balm on her dry lips and combed her hair. I rubbed her feet with lotion. I wept and fought with God, saying yes, saying no, saying please.

She coughed and fought death for six days and nights. The time was both short and endless. Never, to the end and to this day, and in spite of much encouragement, was I convinced I was doing the right thing.

"It's this thing, *time*," I raged at God. "Why did you give us time? It makes us crazy."

Time and God

Of course, to write *time* and *God* into the same sentence is to entertain nonsense or even utter sacrilege. You blaspheme God when you chant such popular phrases as "in God's time" or "God has a different schedule from ours" (besides being nonsense, it's close to blasphemy when you conjure up an image of the One on the throne with a Day Timer, a picture that involves clipboards and computer screens and lackeys running about with scraps of calendars in their hands).

Time has always been fascinating to humans, perhaps because it has that element of mystery about it. If all we have is today, why do we remember yesterday? And will tomorrow come?

The Egyptians realized that the Dog Star in Canis Major, which we call Sirius, rose next to the sun every 365 days, about when the annual inundation of the Nile began. Based on this knowledge, they devised a 365-day calendar that apparently began in 4236 B.C., the earliest recorded year in history. And that day was "today" for all the Egyptians and Hittites and Israelites and whoever else was alive.

Not until somewhat recently, in terms of human history, did people find a need for knowing the time of day. As best we know, five to six thousand years ago great civilizations in the Middle East and North Africa initiated clock making as opposed to calendar making. And I suspect that has been a function of our fallenness; rather than living in the day, we watched clocks. People devised sundials and water clocks and hourglasses that measured small segments of time and taught us to count forward and backward: only an hour ago . . .

God may be in the details, but God still keeps one atom or a million firmly fastened in timelessness. What happened in the Mesozoic is happening now, and what will happen when earth dies is also in God's awareness. But you and I are *in* time, because time—albeit that we sometimes like to describe it as an instrument of the

Enemy—is God's gift to us. In older age, we need to do two things with that time: receive it with reverence and use it sacramentally.

That was the urgency I felt as I hovered over my mother, by then only a tiny lump in the bed. She was never more than five feet tall, and now she seemed to bear the weight of her years by shrinking even more. When I couldn't stand being there, I stood in the doorway and wept, and other residents of the home wheeled by in their chairs, trying not to see me; they had their own struggles with time. Friends came and sat with me and brought me potato chips and Coca-Cola. My son and daughter-in-law came; Mother didn't open her eyes, but she smiled wonderfully when my son whispered his love into her ear. My daughters called, and I held the phone so they could say goodbye and I love you, and she smiled the same way. I kept saying, "I love you, Mother," the way she'd wanted me to say it when I was four and wouldn't.

The doctor increased her morphine; he said she was in pain, but in my heart I called it euthanasia and felt guilty.

Two friends were with me when she died. Her breathing just drifted into silence, and one of my friends took my hand and said, "Our Father, who art in heaven . . ." We prayed and then we got the nurse. My mother's time was done.

Or was it? She was eighty-seven. Is that long enough to live? Or might she have wanted another five or ten years—years, the nurse said grimly, that would have included bedsores and hard physical therapy and increasing mental confusion? But didn't she have a right to those things? Should one person decide when another's time is done?

Time, like hair, thins with age, maybe not by God's design but by humanity's carelessness. I now see the gossamer layers of my own time diminishing around me: I am past sixty, and if I'm ever going to ride in a hot air balloon or learn to tap dance or visit a place where orangutans race free through the undergrowth, I must do it now. But what I want to hear is that there is good news, news that there's always enough time for delight.

Time and Joy

There's a Hindu concept, one that we westerners sometimes struggle to understand, called *ananda*. As I understand it, *ananda* is that essential joy that holds the universe together; and my spirit responds to the idea. Is the world really held together by joy? Then woven into the rope of *ananda* is the utter grace of time, time ripened for joy, time not spent or killed but nurtured and tended.

How do you treat the gift of time as a sacrament? Is a desk an altar, is the dinner table a Eucharist, is your house a temple?

Not always. This morning my husband and I argued about the trash. We were not yet awake while we juggled wastebaskets and sacks and tried to organize the recycling boxes, and he swore at me. In fact, he used a short, unpleasant obscenity that made my cheeks get hot and my already irregular heartbeat go into a second of frenzy. I wanted to have back the moment before he cursed; I wanted the earlier time returned to me. Instead of waiting to see if the sands would run backward, I made a fuss, saying loudly that I did not deserve that language and he had no right to use it. We quarreled for a moment, and then it was too late to snatch back the time. I microwaved a bowl of oatmeal and ate it with no pleasure, gulped a cup of coffee seasoned with rancor. I smacked time and sent it yipping away.

We did not stay mad; I came into my office and started writing, and I could hear the news from his radio in the next room. We called out our opinions about the hurricane and the international situation. I remembered to dash into the utility room to take meat from the freezer so I could make my famous pot roast of pork with cilantro and orange for dinner. He did some laundry. There was no permanent damage.

Or was there? Is the universe damaged by those moments? I can never have those moments back, any more than I can go scrabble at our churchyard garden, where I scattered Mother's ashes, to somehow reassemble her life. God holds out the sacrament of time, and sometimes I turn away to partake of something else. Today my husband and I committed an egregious sin— and this was only an eighteen-second skirmish.

The Epistle to the Hebrews says, "exhort one another every day, as long as it is called 'today,' so that none of you may be hardened by the deceitfulness of sin." Hardened! Deceitfulness! We are hardened to the damage we inflict by the moments we ignore while the day is called "today." And the deceitfulness? It arrives straight from hell, saying, "Time has run out" or "There's plenty of time." Both statements are lies; we, like time, belong to God, who lets us call this "today." Today is what *is*.

Meanwhile, when you look up, God is still holding out time, saying, "Take, eat . . ."

Then here is God's overwhelming demand: that we treat time with the same honor and respect with which we go forward to the altar to receive the Body and Blood. Whether a person believes there are two sacraments or seven, when we multiply them by time, we are seized with an urgency about God that we've never had before. Time is like manna and must be plucked up every day or it rots, and one of humanity's sins is its inability to decide what to do, thereby doing nothing. Not that doing nothing is sinful, at least not so long as you *intentionally* do nothing. But doing nothing because you stand at the crossroads and won't take a step in either direction ignores the time that God holds out for our holy consumption.

I had a chance to do nothing intentionally last weekend. I was at a retreat in the mountains, and as I was loading the car to go home, the rain that falls for about nine months here in Oregon became snow, and I was gripped for a few moments, watching a particular snowflake fall, then rise again in an air current, then fall, rise, fall. Suddenly the spring rain rushed over the snow, turning my uncovered hair into a snarl of curls. And then a rainbow formed.

I rushed indoors, dripping wet, and told those who were dragging their suitcases to the door that if they hurried they might see snow and rainbow at the same time.

Only one woman raced outside, her face full of joy; she stood in the snowfall and gazed at the great shimmering arch of color hanging in the snow. But the others cast about for umbrellas and hooded jackets, muttering that they should have left at lunch, before the last session, so they could have gotten down the hill before the mud started rolling. The word "time" got batted through the air like a badminton birdie.

One man said, "You've seen one rainbow, you've seen them all." I started to argue that some are red on the bottom and some blue-violet, but then I went out and drove away in my car. The rainbow lasted until I turned east, which was about nine minutes—long, in rainbow time.

Time and Covenant

The rainbow is a covenant sign, and covenants require time. The rainbow that appeared after Noah's flood made the amount of time humanly indeterminate and dependent on both divine and natural forces: but floods would never again destroy all life *as long as the earth endures, seedtime and harvest, cold and heat, summer and winter, day and night, shall not cease.* The covenant will last *as long as.* Other covenants also have time constraints; in the wonderful, spooky smokepot covenant with Abraham, God spoke even of the time his descendants would be in captivity. The Ten Commandments were to last as long as the people did. The magic ingredient in each of these agreements is time, in which God remains static and in which we live and move and have our being. God stands at the altar, consecrating time for our use, inviting us to eat the bread of hours and drink the cup of years, urging us to live, to age, even to die, so that time will then propel us into eternity.

Ideas like this make me scared. Will I be asked to stand somewhere timeless and account for every nanosecond of my personal time? Will the very presence of infinity be enough to erase my sins and make me fit for heaven, or will I still be standing, ten billion years from now, reciting the last six days of Mother's life, or the last sixty-some years of mine?

I read recently about a beautiful yellow butterfly that lives only six days. Its time is ripe for dying as soon as it emerges from the chrysalis, so it has to use its fecundity and joy in what is hardly a heartbeat. Somewhere, such a butterfly lived its whole life while Mother died. It drank the whole cup of God's merciless, loving sacrament of time, while my mother grew less and less, and then its life was done. And so was hers.

And if time really is a sacrament, then as we came to the end of the millennium we should have had some sort of hope and joy ready for the next one. I am reminded of the days when I used to teach piano and would try to persuade the children not to stop at the measure bars. "These are signals to start counting again," I would tell them. "Green lights to see what's ahead." The millennium was only a measure bar in time. We have a green light in this century to play with greater delight, to work with a more divine fervor, to hand out joy like candy, to fight for the homeless, to laugh without restraint, to take part in the spiritual formation of our grandchildren, to spend more Octobers planting daffodil bulbs and more Februaries gathering edible field greens. We have this century to live life as we're living it—but with the added element of consciousness.

It is the consciousness of time's sacramental nature that adds intentional holiness to cracking nuts or watermarking paper or straining yogurt or writing a poem. You don't have to suddenly become a new person or change your whole way of being. But now you have to be aware of God's participation in your life. I think that when Jesus told us, "Watch," he may have meant, "Stay alert for the signs of my coming," but he also meant, "Stay alert for the signs of my presence now, in everything you do."

That means that as we consume the sacrament of time in the spirit of holiness, we will still age and die, but we will also take a new spirit into the next life. We start now: using our time for prayer and praying while we use the time in other ways. We engage the idea of death, but we hang onto the promise of resurrection. We let go of the world and reach desperately for God. The time is ripe for joy, and joy holds the universe together.

The feast is almost over, and Jesus is hovering over the wine jars. The best wine is that which is served at the end. We must find our joy in whatever time we have left, in the mighty rushing wind that pervades work, in the Spirit's brooding over the waters of our eating and sleeping, in the crucifixion of wasted hours and the hope of resurrection for those minutes that are redeemed, and finally, joy in that infinitesimal second of death. Because the moments we have as human beings are shaping us for heaven, on a day called "today."

Suggested Reading

BOOKS ABOUT AGING

Cohen, Gene D. *The Creative Age: Waking Human Potential in the Second Half of Life*. New York: Avon Books, 2000.

Fischer, Kathleen R. *Winter Grace: Spirituality and Aging*. Nashville: Upper Room Books, 1998.

McKhann, Guy M., and Marilyn Albert. *Keep Your Brain Young: The Complete Guide to Physical and Emotional Health and Longevity*. New York: John Wiley & Sons, 2002.

Snowdon, David. *Aging with Grace: What the Nun Study Teaches Us about Leading Longer, Healthier, and More Meaningful Lives*. New York: Bantam Books, 2001.

Terkel, Studs. *Will the Circle Be Unbroken? Reflections on Death, Rebirth, and Hunger for a Faith.* New York: New Press, 2001.

Vaillant, George E. *Aging Well: Surprising Guideposts to a Happier Life from the Landmark Harvard Study of Adult Development.* Boston: Little, Brown and Company, 2002.

SOME CHRISTIAN CLASSICS

Francis de Sales, St. *Introduction to the Devout Life.* New York: Vintage Books, 2002.

Kierkegaard, Søren. *Fear and Trembling.* Translated by Alastair Hannay. New York: Viking Penguin, 1985.

Lawrence of the Resurrection, Brother. *Practice of the Presence of God.* Edited by Harold J. Chadwick. North Brunswick, N.J.: Bridge-Logos Publishers, 1999.

Lewis, C. S. *Mere Christianity.* San Francisco: Harper-SanFrancisco, 2001.

Teresa of Ávila, St. *The Interior Castle.* Translated by E. Allison Peers. Garden City, N.Y.: Image Books, 1972.

Thomas à Kempis. *The Imitation of Christ.* Edited and translated by Joseph N. Tylenda, S.J. New York: Vintage Books, 1998.

Scriptures for Lectio Divina

Psalm 71:9
Do not cast me off in the time of old age;
  do not forsake me when my strength is spent.

Psalm 71:18–19
So even to old age and gray hairs,
  O God, do not forsake me,
until I proclaim your might
  to all the generations to come.
Your power and your righteousness, O God
  reach the high heavens.

Psalm 92:12–15
The righteous flourish like the palm tree,
  and grow like a cedar in Lebanon.
They are planted in the house of the LORD*;*
  they flourish in the courts of our God.
In old age they still produce fruit;
  they are always green and full of sap,

showing that the LORD *is upright;*
  he is my rock, and there is no unrighteousness in
  him.

Isaiah 46:4

Even to your old age I am he,
  even when you turn gray I will carry you.
I have made, and I will bear;
  I will carry and will save.

Ruth 4:15

He shall be to you a restorer of life and a nourisher of
your old age; for your daughter-in-law who loves
you, who is more to you than seven sons, has borne
him.

Job 14:7–9

For there is hope for a tree,
  if it is cut down, that it will sprout again,
and that its shoots will not cease.
Though its root grows old in the earth,
  and its stump dies in the ground,
yet at the scent of water it will bud
  and put forth branches like a young plant.

Zechariah 8:4–5

Thus says the LORD *of hosts: Old men and old*
women shall again sit in the streets of Jerusalem, each
with staff in hand because of their great age. And the
streets of the city shall be full of boys and girls play-
ing in its streets.

Psalm 18:46
The LORD lives! Blessed be my rock,
and exalted be the God of my salvation.

Psalm 1:1–3
Happy are those
who do not follow the advice of the wicked,
or take the path that sinners tread,
or sit in the seat of scoffers;
but their delight is in the law of the LORD,
and on his law they meditate day and night.
They are like trees
planted by streams of water,
which yield their fruit in its season,
and their leaves do not wither.
In all that they do, they prosper.

Psalm 8:1
O LORD, our Sovereign,
how majestic is your name in all the earth!
You have set your glory above the heavens.

Psalm 150
Praise the LORD!
Praise God in his sanctuary;
praise him in his mighty firmament!
Praise him for his mighty deeds;
praise him according to his surpassing greatness!
Praise him with trumpet sound;
praise him with lute and harp!

Praise him with tambourine and dance;
  praise him with strings and pipe!
Praise him with clanging cymbals;
  praise him with loud clashing cymbals!
Let everything that breathes praise the LORD!
Praise the LORD!

Index

A

Abimelech, 84

Abraham, 180, 253

acedia, sin of, 27–28

Adam, 122

Adams, Douglas, 18

Adams, James Truslow, 217

addiction, 191

afterlife. *See also* Resurrection
  belief in, wavering, 17–18, 19
  living life as if a believer, 19

Agee, James, 119

aging
  colorful foods to slow process of,
    66–67
  community, seeking as we age,
    148–49 (*see also* community)
  fear of, 31
  financial worries associated with, 27
  following Christ during, 175–76
  forgiveness as an ease to, 173 (*see also*
    forgiveness)
  friendships, 150–51
  God, inviting into life in later years,
    26–30
  guilt feelings associated with (*see*
    guilt)
  humiliations of, 34–35
  peace accompanying, 64
  perception of others, 34–35

physical limitations, 5, 27, 28–29,
  32–34, 44

process of, 13–14

psychological process of, 61–62

reaching out, 200, 201–6

separateness, avoiding, 150

sex in later life (*see* sex)

sleep difficulties (*see* sleep)

spiritual beauty, clothing oneself in,
  35–36

spirituality of, 5–6

suffering, as a way to share Christ's
  suffering, 41

tension of, 127–28

AIDS, condemnation of victim of,
  9–10

Al Qaeda, 147

al-'Arabi, Ibn, 37

ananda, 267–68

Angelica, Sister (Catholic TV host), 109

angels, jurisdiction of, 139

anger, 49. *See also* bitterness
  getting in touch with, 52
  God, directed toward, 163–64, 166
  parents, directed toward, 171–73

Anselm, St., 133

Anthony, St., 82

antioxidants, 91

anxiety
  letting go, as release of, 55
  Psalms on, 78